...with a beautiful person, may God Continue to Bless you,

Dr. Ruby J. Harvey

Trials,
Tribulations,
and Blessings
of a Prophetess

PALMETTO
P U B L I S H I N G
Charleston, SC
www.PalmettoPublishing.com

Paperback ISBN: 9798822960015
eBook ISBN: 9798822960022

Trials, Tribulations, and Blessings of a Prophetess

DR. RUBY J. HARVEY

Table of Contents

Introduction

The Spirit of the Lord dropped this subject in my spirit about two years ago. The original idea was titled "Meeting with the Prophetic," and I held onto it, thinking that one day it would be a book, but He didn't tell me to write it yet.

I lost my husband in October of 2023. After his service, things began to happen concerning this subject. At the repast, one of my sisters in the Lord, whom I grew up with, told me that God wanted me to keep writing. I heard her plainly, but at that time, I couldn't collect my thoughts to understand that God was using her. She was the first of seven messengers God sent to tell me to write the book. One of them called to check on me and prayed for me. After she hung up the phone, she called right back. I asked her if that was a pocket call.

She said no and asked, "Are you writing a book?"

I said, "No, I'm not. I have one, but God hasn't told me to write it."

She said, "God wants you to write it, and it's going to bless a lot of people."

After she called, five more people confirmed that the Lord wanted me to write the book or asked point-blank, "Have you started the book yet?" I'd never told any of them that I had a book thought from God. Five of my spiritual sisters and two brothers, one of them being my own son and another my sister-in-law, gave me this message. My sister-in-law, who was here in St. Louis and had just returned to Memphis, called me and stated that when she was here and asleep on the recliner, she dreamed that I was supposed to write a book.

Eventually, I put my hand on my chest and said, "Lord, I can't take it," but I knew He would give me the strength to do it. I was feeling very nervous about it, but because of the seven witnesses, it gave me a feeling of urgency. The Bible says in Matthew 18:16 "Out of the mouth of two or three witnesses, every word shall be established."

About four decades ago, there was a man of God, a prophet, who was invited to come to our church to minister. I came in late that evening, and he was in the heat of his message. I came with the expectations to receive a blessing. I hadn't been seated very long before he said, "Everybody bow your heads, let us pray."

While my head was bowed, I heard the Spirit say, "He's going to call you out," but I continued to be involved in the prayer.

I had on a red dress and a red hat. The prophet lifted his head, looked to the area where I was sitting, pointed, and said, "Lady in red, come down here."

I turned around with everyone else, pointed to myself, and whispered, "Me?"

He said, "Yes, you."

I went down to the altar, and he prophesied that God had something great for me and was going to do great things through me. Then he asked me, "Do you want it?"

I said, "Yes, sir."

This message was the beginning of everything I experienced thereafter. Since then, here and there, I've seen and experienced the prophecy come to pass. Still today, more of the things he said are happening. When the Lord gave me this book subject, I felt led to look him up and found out that he had just passed away. I was saddened to hear that he was no longer among us, but I'll always remember his prophecy to me. It shows us that whatever words the Lord has spoken over you, in due season, they will come to pass.

Prayerfully, with my history of trials, tribulations, and blessings, I hope to help you and strengthen you where you need it, and increase your faith and emotional and physical healing. God will often send people ahead of us to suffer things and learn how to endure them to help others live. We must make up our minds that we're not going to miss Jesus for anything or anybody. As God has been faithful to us, we must learn to be faithful to Him.

As I began to write and show how the Lord was leading me, it felt miraculous because, without the Lord, there was no way humanly possible I could have remembered all of these stories and experiences (many of them over four decades of living) to share with people who have walked a similar road. Most of the stories and experiences that happened helped me to understand how to love God with all of my heart, soul, and mind, and my neighbor as myself, even while suffering and to learn to follow what the Word of God says (Matthew 22:37–39). With this revelation I knew that this qualified me to work for the Lord, because if I say I love God but can't stand the people that Jesus gave His life for, then I'm not ready to do the work of God. It's much more than looking the part with my gifts.

A lot of us have been stuck in life like a car stuck in the mud, but the Lord wants us to grow and stop blaming other people, by living according to the Word of God. When we fail, we must repent and get back on track. We're all different, we look different and act differently, but God loves us all the same. He's given us all different abilities or gifts to operate in His Kingdom. He will teach us how to operate in the gifts that He's given us. The most valuable thing is to use our gifts to help others. On our journey, we will meet some prophetic messengers God has sent to us to encourage and reassure us that whatever we're going through and whatever is hurting us, is going to change, and it won't always be like this. A prophetic message points to the future, but it will always give you hope. God wants us to listen to our dreams, learn through our experiences, and do good to all people as our Lord Jesus did.

PART ONE

PROPHETIC DREAMS

Chapter One

THE SILVER TREE AND THE PROMISE OF SALVATION

I had a dream about a decade before I was saved. There was a huge tree that reached far into the sky. It was silver and had many gifts on it. The gifts were of different sizes and colors, and they were so beautiful. Then I heard a voice say, "All of these gifts are yours." I began to rejoice and leap up and down. The voice continued, "You will receive them, but not now." At that time, I didn't know how to interpret the dream, but I had enough insight to know that this dream was from God, telling me about my future. But it would come to pass in another season.

A lot of people struggle in their lives, trying to survive emotionally because they don't understand the cards life has dealt them. I was one of those people. But I noticed that many times when life was unbearable and I didn't know what to do or which way to turn. The Lord did something or sent someone with the answers, I didn't know how to pray for it at that time. It doesn't matter if you're single or married with a family; everyone has a story, even if they never share it.

The beautiful silver tree with all the colorful gifts never left my mind. Later on in life, as I viewed my status at that time, I decided that some things had to change. I began to seek the Lord as best as I understood by praying and asking God what I should do to make my life better. The Lord started sending people who carried themselves as if they had the Salvation I was looking for, and I would ask them questions. Somewhere along the way, I heard that I needed to receive the Holy Ghost to be saved. I asked a pastor's wife what the Holy Ghost was, as I wasn't reading my Bible yet.

The lady said to me, "You know when you're in the kitchen cooking a pot of food?"

I said, "Yes."

She said, "When you taste it and hear a little voice say you need just a little more salt?"

I said, "Yes, I've heard that." Then I asked, "Is that the Holy Ghost?" And she said, "Yes."

I said "I didn't know that was the Holy Ghost; I have heard that."

I found out later that was not the Spirit of God. That was my own spirit telling me to put more salt in the pot.

As I moved on, I met more people who knew more about God and had a relationship with Him. More and more, I was able to connect the dots on receiving Jesus in my life as my Savior, Lord, and Christ.

The big day happened on August 11, 1978. The gift of Salvation is so real. When I asked God to save me, I realized that it was personal. I asked God to save me on my birthday, which was August 16th. He's so gracious and miraculous. He came through for me as I asked Him, but like a great father, He showed up five days early. My Salvation was so powerful that it wiped away my appetite. I was so overwhelmed with joy from being filled with the Holy Spirit that I lost six pounds that week. I know everyone's story is different, but this is my personal Salvation story. The thing that matters to the Lord is that we show up when He calls us, and everybody's story isn't the same.

As life continued, I noticed gifts operating in the Spirit, such as laying hands on people who were demon possessed and casting the demons out in the name of Jesus. I also observed praying for the blind and seeing their eyes opened, praying for people with breast cancer, and witnessing their healing. Now I understood and connected the dots to the big silver tree with all the beautiful gifts. I found that the Lord will deal with each of us in a way that we can understand so we can move on through life with the gifts He's given us. God knows how to deal with us as individuals to get us where we need to be in this life. He'll continue to teach us everything we need to know to be prepared to meet Him when He returns for His people.

In Matthew 16:15, Jesus instructs His disciples about Salvation.

In verse 17, He told them that signs would follow the believer: "In my name shall they cast out devils; they shall speak with new tongues."

Verse 18 says, "They shall lay hands on the sick, and they shall recover."

Everything that the Lord has purposed for our life will come to pass if we believe it.

STATEMENTS OF TRUTH

The Lord showed me my Salvation years before He actually brought it to pass. I know that people, in general, are different, and God deals with us differently and in ways that we can understand, because I knew exactly what the dream meant. I was very clear that this would happen, but it would be a future event. The Lord loves us so much that He wants all of His people to be saved and to know Him. As we begin to read the Bible, we find out how He feels about us and how He feels about sin.

John 3:16 tells us, "For God so loved the world, that He gave His only begotten Son, that whosoever believeth in Him should not perish, but have everlasting life."

There were so many things that I didn't know, such as Romans 5:8: "But God commendeth His love toward us, in that, while we were yet sinners, Christ died for us."

When I began to read the Scriptures, I took it personally, as though it was talking directly to me. Scriptures like Romans 3:23) which says, "For all have sinned, and come short of the glory of God," and Romans 6:23: "For the wages of sin is death; but the gift of God is eternal life through Jesus Christ our Lord."

As I continued to read the things that the Lord wanted me to know, I read 2 Peter 1:3–13, which summarized for me the things that God wanted me to know:

"According as His divine power hath given unto us all things that pertain unto life and godliness, through the knowledge of him that hath called us to glory and virtue:

Whereby are given unto us exceeding great and precious promises that by these you might be partakers of the divine nature, having escaped the corruption that is in the world through lust.

And beside this, giving all diligence, add to your faith virtue; and to virtue knowledge;

And to knowledge temperance; and to temperance patience; and to patience godliness;

And to godliness brotherly kindness; and to brotherly kindness charity.

For if these things be in you, and abound, they make you that ye shall neither be barren nor unfruitful in the knowledge of our Lord Jesus Christ."

2 Peter 3:9–10 also reads:

"The Lord is not slack concerning his promise, as some men count slackness; but is longsuffering to us-ward, not willing that any should perish, but that all should come to repentance.

But the day of the Lord will come as a thief in the night; in which the heavens shall pass away with a great noise, and the elements shall melt with fervent heat, the earth also and the works that are therein shall be burned up."

There are many Scriptures that point to God's love toward His people. As for me, I believed what I was reading and what God was revealing, and I wanted to know Him. I believe the Scriptures that tell us that He loved us so much that He came into this world to die on a cross for us (John 3:16–17). Although He was innocent and never did anything wrong or committed any sins, because of His love for us, He died in our place. He allowed us to be born again by being sorrowful for our sins and repenting for our evil deeds. For those who say they never did evil deeds, we were all in the same sinful condition. David said in Psalm 51:5, "Behold, I was shapen in iniquity; and in sin did my mother conceive me." We all inherited a sin nature after Adam and Eve sinned in the Garden of Eden as described in Genesis chapter 3. If we continue to choose to live in sin and reject God, the reward for doing that is death. But if we accept His gift, which is eternal life through Jesus Christ our Lord, we find that God is such a loving and merciful God. Therefore, we should continue to give Him thanks for all that He's done, just as the Psalmist did:

> Psalm 136:1–3 says:
> "O give thanks unto the Lord; for He is good: for His mercy endureth forever.
> O give thanks unto the God of gods: for His mercy endureth forever.
> O give thanks to the Lord of lords: for His mercy endureth forever."

Chapter Two

VISIONS OF WARNING AND PROTECTION

I had a dream that my mother-in-law's house caught on fire and was burning with high flames. After a few days, I told my husband that I needed to call her to make sure she was all right. When I called her, she didn't mention anything until I told her about the dream. Then she said, "Yesterday, I was walking up the pathway. As I got closer, I saw dark smoke coming out of the house, and it frightened me so badly; not only was the house on fire, but my mother was in the house. I didn't know if she was trapped or not. When I came closer, I saw my mother outside on her knees, crying, because there were valuables in the house that were being destroyed in the fire. The house burned to the ground, and everything was destroyed, but my mother was safe."

Remember this: bad things sometimes happen to good people, but know that God doesn't do things to hurt us. Some things happen to us because of the circumstances we are in. Sometimes bad things happen because of the people we choose as friends. It's a good idea to stay prayerful so that the Lord can show us hidden dangers we can avoid and be covered. The thing I learned from a story like this is that God will give people gifts even if they don't know Him. I had the gift of dreaming things that came to pass before my Salvation. Romans 11:29 says, "For the gifts and calling of God are without repentance." From our birth, the Lord already knew how He would use each of us, and the devil knew also. That's why he seeks to destroy those whom God has predestined (Romans 8:29).

STATEMENTS OF TRUTH

1. Sometimes God will warn us of things that will come to pass to prepare us for the unknown.
2. The Lord is never the cause of bad things that come our way because He loves His people; He'll always be there as He promised: "I will never leave you nor forsake you." Hebrews 13:5

Chapter Three

THE DREAM OF THE SNAKE AND THE LESSONS OF TRUST

I dreamed about a snake in my house. In the dream, the snake was crawling through my house and disappeared. I awakened the next morning to a song in the atmosphere: "My road sure gets a little rocky on my way home." I had heard the song before, so I was very familiar with it. As I laid in bed, I meditated on the dream and wondered what it meant. I also remembered in the dream that some people came to help me find the snake, but it was nowhere to be found. Someone pulled out a shiny hoe that's used in the South to chop cotton or work in the garden. A voice came from one of the saints and said, "Put the hoe up, it's not time to use the hoe."

The Word of God teaches us in 2 Corinthians 10:4–5, "For the weapons of our warfare are not carnal, but mighty through God to the pulling down of strong holds; Casting down imaginations and every high thing that exalteth itself against the knowledge of God, and bringing into captivity every thought to the obedience of Christ." The Lord didn't answer me a word about the dream, but I knew He was telling me through the song that some rocky trouble was coming. Not many days after the dream, trouble showed up: "They say you did this and you did that, and you said this and you said that." Yes, I was devastated by all of those untrue statements. But God had taught me that when you can't defend yourself, keep silent, pray, and watch.

I didn't ask the Lord why this had happened because He had warned me about it in the dream. I received the dream as an understanding that the Lord God knew this would happen to me before it happened. He would surely cover me in the situation and deliver me out of it. I could have gotten angry, and to a degree, I'm sure I was, but I thank God that I didn't act out in anger. I don't remember asking God why, although I didn't believe that He'd done this to me. He knew it beforehand because He's omniscient and knows all things. He was there to share it with me or to warn me because He's omnipresent. The warning kept me from getting out of character. Know this: believers can get out of character and act a fool when troubles come.

I wouldn't go as far as to say we're not saved when any of us do this; we just haven't learned to control our human spirit. The following is a list of lessons that we learn from Ephesians 4:21–32. As you have heard and have been taught by Jesus, this is the way you should respond to His teaching:

1. Put off the old self, the way you used to be.
2. Change your mind to the things of Christ by becoming a new person.
3. Be the new person created after God in righteousness and true holiness.
4. Stop all lies and tell the truth to everyone because we are members of one another.
5. If we're angry from sun up to sundown, it is sinful; it's no longer anger, it is wrath. We can't stay close to God and be full of wrath.
6. Don't allow the devil any foothold in your life.
7. Don't go back to stealing and doing wrong. Work with your hands and do good, helping others when they need it.
8. Stop corrupt speech from your lips. Speak only those good things that build up and edify so that those who hear you will be blessed.
9. Never grieve the Holy Spirit of God by doing the opposite of what His Word says.

In everything I've gone through He was right there. Always remember that whatever negative situation you find yourself in, if God allowed you to come to it, He will definitely bring you through it. And eventually, everything will work for your good because the Word of God says so in Romans 8:28. The Lord allows us to be tested. He'll sometimes give us a warning. It will show us how well we know the Lord and how we apply knowing the Scriptures. Ephesians 4 shows us how we should and shouldn't be in situations now that we know Jesus. Romans 8:1 says, "There is therefore now no condemnation to them which are in Christ Jesus, who walk not after the flesh, but after the Spirit."

This story is a reminder of how God allows us to go through things, and He never breaks a situation down to us. Even when a situation is very painful, He wants us to trust Him through it all. When we go through things in life, the Scriptures say it's going to work for our good (Romans 8:28). I'm thinking of Daniel chapter 6 where we read that Daniel had an excellent spirit and the king set him over the whole realm of presidents and princes. "Then the presidents and princes sought to find occasion against Daniel concerning the kingdom; but they could find no occasion nor fault; forasmuch as he was faithful, neither was there any error or fault found in him" (Dan 6:4). The wise men knew Daniel prayed to God, so they tricked the king into making a decree, a new law that anyone who prayed to any god would be thrown into the lions' den. But Daniel prayed to God anyway: "Then these men assembled and found Daniel praying and making supplication before his God" (Dan 6:11).

Only God knows why people choose to mistreat others. According to the Word of God, only those of us who don't grow in certain areas can be used by the enemy. If those things were reversed back on the accusers, they would not be able to handle it. My understanding of this story is that I must take personal responsibility for all of my actions and be accountable to God, because one day we will all have to leave this world. We must be in right standing with God and with people when we leave. We must watch how we act and react when tested, because someone is watching us go through it.

STATEMENTS OF TRUTH

1. Whatever God allows to come into your life that's negative, there's always a lesson to be learned.
2. The Lord already knows who will trust Him.
3. Whenever you're plotted on, do nothing on your own. Do as Daniel did—pray and wait on God.

Chapter Four

A CALL FROM HEAVEN: MY MOTHER'S JOURNEY TO SALVATION

Around 1981, about the time my youngest child was born, I dreamed I was talking to my mom on a long-distance phone call. We got disconnected, and I tried to call her back, but the call failed. I kept trying to call her back, and I finally reached her.

She said, "I want to tell you something."

"What is it?" I asked.

She said, "I don't have too much longer to live."

The news made me very sad. I woke up sad and wondered what that meant.

Not long after that dream, my mom called me and said she was ready to know the Lord Jesus. From then on, I began to talk to her about Jesus. I sent her Scriptures about Salvation, and the death, burial, and resurrection of Jesus Christ. I also sent her a book about the Rapture, showing that at the Lord's return, some people will not be ready. After reading the book, Mom called me and said, "I need Salvation now because I want to be ready when Jesus comes back for His people." I remembered the Scripture in John 6:44: "No man can come to me, except the Father which hath sent me draw him," meaning all of us who come to Jesus don't come on our own; the Father Himself draws us to Jesus.

STATEMENTS OF TRUTH

1. The Father is the one who draws people to Jesus. (John 6:44). According to the testimony of many people, the Father causes them to think about their troubled lives. It brings conviction of their wrong living and guides them to make the right decisions in their lives and to accept Jesus as their Lord and Savior, which puts them in the position to be ready to go with the Lord when He returns for His Church.

My mother was born again in 1981. She lived for the Lord until He called her home in 2016. 2 Peter 3:9 says, "The Lord is not slack concerning his promise, as some men count slackness; but is longsuffering to us-ward, not willing that any should perish, but that all should come to repentance." Hebrews 9:27 says, "And as it is appointed unto men once to die, but after this the judgment." God will always give us the grace to come to Him and accept Him as our Savior and Lord before we leave this world.

I give God the praise for showing my mom that she needed Him, and by the grace of God, she accepted Him and lived for Him until she went home to be with Him. God does not show favoritism. He will save all who comes to Him if they ask. He will also heal and deliver them according to His will.

Chapter Five

THE WARNING DREAM AND WORKPLACE ADVERSARIES

I dreamed of some policemen. In my dream, I went into a store to get something, and some policemen were in different aisles. I noticed that one of them was watching me as if I had stolen something, but I had just entered the store. I couldn't focus on what I came in the store to get because one of the cops kept staring at me. I decided to leave the store because it made me feel uncomfortable. As I left the store, I sped up my steps to a fast walk. By that time, one of the cops came to the door, pulled out his gun, and began to shoot at me. I ran fast and hard, and he kept shooting at me. On the last shot, he hit a billboard sign. When I woke up, I asked the Lord what that was all about. He walked me through the dream and told me it was about the place of employment where He had sent me to work. He showed me the enemies at that job who were against me because some of them didn't like the skills I used on the job. They were trying to work undercover to get rid of me. They represented bosses and managers. They were working undercover to destroy me because they knew that the big boss liked my work and would never get rid of me without a reason. God gave me the dream to warn me of the harm they desired to do to me.

STATEMENTS OF TRUTH

1. This story shows that as long as you live as a believer, God will always give His people assignments to do. Some people will not like that you were the one God chose for the assignment. If we're really living the way the Lord calls for us to live, though, sometimes you will have problems with other people. But remember Scripture statements like this:

2. 2 Timothy 3:12 says, "Yea, and all that will live godly in Christ Jesus shall suffer persecution."

1 Peter 3:8 says, "Finally, be ye all of one mind, having compassion one of another. Love as brethren, be pitiful, be courteous."

And verse 9 tells us that rendering evil for evil or railing for railing puts us out of the will of God.

"For he that would love life and see good days, let him refrain his tongue from evil, and his lips that they speak no guile. Let him eschew evil, meaning keep away from evil, and do good. Let him seek peace and ensue it. For the eyes of the Lord are over the righteous, and His ears are open unto their prayers, but the face of the Lord is against them that do evil. And who is he that will harm you if ye be followers of that which is good?" (2 Pet 3:10–13)

Peter's letter shows us how to endure suffering through persecution of any kind, no matter what's going on in our lives. Jesus said, "If ye continue in my word, then are ye my disciples indeed. And ye shall know the truth, and the truth shall make you free" (John 8:31-32)

Chapter Six

A WEDDING DREAM AND A FATHER'S FAREWELL

I dreamed I married a short little man. In the dream, I was preparing to get married. Honestly, the dream felt weird because I was trying to figure out what was going on since, in reality, I was already married. As the dream proceeded, I was on the dance floor dancing with the short man, but I couldn't see his face. I was trying to figure out who this person was. That was the basis of the dream. The wedding gown that I wore was such a beautiful white dress and the prettiest white shoes that I had ever seen.

A little time went by, and I was at a visiting church assembly. Someone came and told me my father had passed away. I began to feel so sad and disturbed over the news.

After traveling for my father's service, we returned home, and a few days later, I went to the mall with some relatives. They asked me if I wanted to go into some stores, but I said no, I was going to find a seat and wait. While I was sitting there, I asked the Lord what that dream meant. He unfolded the dream to me immediately as I listened. He said, "I was preparing you for your father's death." My father had received the Lord Jesus a while before he had passed, and he was saved. The Lord was revealing that information to me. The beautiful white wedding gown represented the Church, and my father danced with the bride, which was me in the dream. I couldn't see his face because the Lord hid it from me until it was time. I rejoiced because I knew that the Lord wanted me to know that my father had died in the Lord.

The Lord, being omniscient, always knows everything. However, in this serious matter, He camouflaged my dad's death until I actually got the news of it. There was absolutely no way that I could have figured out the dream on my own and understood the revelation before my dad passed away. He was five feet four inches tall, he weighed about 130 pounds, and he wore size 29-29 pants. He was a very petite man and very funny at times, keeping his friends happy with laughter. About a year or two before he passed, I had the opportunity to introduce him to Jesus. I'm still thankful that he accepted the call to Salvation. Jesus knows everything. When Lazarus was sick, Jesus stayed away on purpose, knowing that Lazarus would die. But it was all done for the glory of God because He knows everything. He always knows what He'll do.

STATEMENTS OF TRUTH

1. One thing we know is that one day we will leave this world. Hebrews 9:27 says, "And it is appointed unto men once to die."
2. We will leave this world through death or through the Rapture of the Church when we are caught up to meet the Lord (1 Thessalonians 4:16).
3. It is important for us to be ready at all times.
4. It is important not to miss the opportunity to witness to others about Jesus.
5. My dad accepted the Lord Jesus before he passed away.

Chapter Seven

THE LOUD NOISE AND THE JOURNEY TO SPIRITUAL GROWTH

When I was very young in Christ Jesus, I dreamed that there was a loud noise in my house. As I heard this loud noise and tried to find out where it was coming from, I went toward the basement. It was getting louder and louder. I reached the basement stairs and slowly went down the steps, feeling fear-stricken. As I drew closer, I discovered that it was my washing machine making the loud noise. The top of the machine was popping loudly. All of a sudden, I saw big rusty bolts and screws coming out of the laundry. When I woke up, I asked the Lord what that dream meant. The Lord told me, "I saved you and gave you My Spirit, but you don't know Me. You must study the Word of God and learn who I am and what I want from you."

"Oh Lord, help me Jesus!" Learning this life isn't just about saying that we believe and walking through life without paying attention to our character, the way we act, and how we treat other people. The Word of God is the living Word. I've learned by reading it, studying it, and meditating on it. It produces great benefits. It must be our spiritual life.

For example, the first thing I realized when I was born again of the water and of the Spirit, according to the story of Jesus and Nicodemus in John 3, is that the Lord knows exactly how to get His people to the place of Salvation. Acts 2 tells the story of the Lord's plan for the Church for Salvation. After desiring to be saved, the Lord came into my life on August 11, 1978, by filling me with His Spirit. I was so full of joy after receiving Jesus into my life, it literally took away my appetite, as I previously stated, I lost six pounds that week thinking about the goodness of God and praising Him, thanking Him, and meditating on Him. My personal experience was mind-blowing. I understand that everybody's experience isn't the same. The main thing is to know and understand God for yourself.

What the Lord revealed to me was that getting saved was a great move on my part, but that wasn't all of it. I needed to learn who this great God was who saved me when I asked Him to, I needed to know what He required of me. I needed to know how to spend the rest of my life and what my assignments were as a new believer. I read 1 Peter 2:1–2, "Wherefore laying aside all malice, and all guile, and hypocrisies, and envies, and all evil speakings, as newborn babes, desire the sincere milk of the word, that ye may grow thereby."

STATEMENTS OF TRUTH

After being born again, our lives are not over; we must continue in His Word by continuing to grow spiritually. When I asked the Lord what the dream meant, He revealed through the dream that after He saved me and gave me His Spirit, I had to study the Word of God, meditate on it, and it would cause me to be delivered in my own spirit of things that don't please God. I know that's what we're taught in the Word of God, showing that we must continue to strive to be like God.

Scriptures like Ephesians 4, as stated before, shows us things about the old person we were before Salvation. We can't stay there anymore. Paul names a list of negative things that believers should not do and not allow them to be a part of our lives anymore. He also gave a list of positive things we should do. We already know these things, but because it is written, it gives us more hope to follow the Word of God. If the Lord doesn't want it, I don't want it either.

We must grow spiritually to be an effective witness in the Kingdom of God. As we grow spiritually, Ephesians 4 is a good place to start. The chapter shows us how to get rid of things concerning our old life, such as:

Our old way of doing things, "which is corrupt, are the things that we should get rid of. We're invited to be renewed in the spirit of our minds" (4:22).

"Let all bitterness and wrath and anger and clamor and evil speaking be put away from you, with all malice: And be ye kind one to another, tenderhearted, forgiving one another, even as God for Christ's sake hath forgiven you" (4:31–32)

The first thing to know after our conversion is that because you have been born again, you are filled with the Holy Spirit of God, and you are a new person. 2 Corinthians 5:17 says, "Therefore if any man be in Christ, he is a new creature: old things are passed away; behold, all things are become new."

Chapter Eight

THE LINE OF SAINTS AND THE TEST OF FAITH

I dreamed I was in line with a lot of people dressed in white. It was a very long line of people, and because they were all dressed in white, I assumed they were saints. I was somewhere in the middle of the line, wondering why we were lined up and dressed in white. While thinking on these things, I stepped out of line to look down the front of the line to see what was going on. I was devastated by what I saw—it was a guillotine. The guillotine was a device consisting of two poles and a blade in which a person was beheaded. After I saw this, I realized the saints were going through the line to be beheaded. I was devastated and moved further back in the line so that I wouldn't reach the front too fast. While moving backward, it actually looked weird because in the dream, I could see how my response to that knowledge looked. Then I heard a voice speak to me and say, "It doesn't matter if you're number ten or twenty, you still have to go through." After I heard the voice, I stood up like a soldier and kept moving forward until it was my time to step up to the guillotine. They hit the handle, the blade came down, and I woke up.

STATEMENTS OF TRUTH

Jesus was persecuted before His death; believers will be persecuted too, and persecution can destroy people if we don't understand it through the Word of God. No one can escape it. It must be reciprocated back in love, because most of the time it comes to us through other people. The Bible tells us that, "God chastens those that He loves and scourges every son whom He receives" (Heb 12:6).

I was a young believer when I had this dream. Younger believers—and sometimes older believers too—don't understand the concept of suffering or being persecuted. But the truth of it is written in the Word of God. 2 Timothy 3:12 says, "Yea, and all that will live godly in Christ Jesus shall suffer persecution." We all go through things, but when we understand what the Word of God is instructing us to do through persecutions, we must follow it.

Jesus was persecuted before His death. Isaiah 53:7, states, "He was oppressed and He was afflicted, yet he opened not his mouth: He is brought as a lamb to the slaughter and as a sheep before her shearers is dumb, so He opened not His mouth." The Lord was showing me through my dream that there is no escaping persecution. When we live for Him, we will be tested periodically in our lifetime. We can decide if we're going to be a strong believers and learn to trust God in every situation, or we will continue to be prey for the devil, giving up around every corner. Remember, nothing can save us but believing what the Word of God says and obeying what it says. Nothing can keep us from continuing to believe in the Word of God. And when you're persecuted, meditate and practice building your faith.

1. Jesus said, "I am the way, the truth, and the life" (John 14:6).
2. "Come unto me all ye that labor and are heavy laden, and I will give you rest. Take my yoke upon you and learn of me, for I am meek and lowly in heart, and you shall find rest unto your souls." (Matt 11:28–29).
3. "Casting all your care upon Him; for He careth for you" (1 Pet 5:7).
4. "Then said Jesus unto his disciples, 'If any man will come after me, let him deny himself and take up his cross and follow me'" (Matt 16:24).
5. Hebrews 11 shows us the perfect examples of faith and continuance. The people described in this chapter are called the heroes of faith. They endured suffering and hardship, yet they held on to their faith in God, which allowed them to achieve the victory.
6. "Looking unto Jesus, the author and finisher of our faith; who for the joy that was set before him endured the cross, despising the shame, and is set down at the right hand of the throne of God" (Heb 12:2).
7. "For whom the Lord loveth, he chasteneth and scourgeth every son whom he receive" (Heb 12:6).
8. "Now no chastening for the present seemeth to be joyous, but grievous: nevertheless afterward it yieldeth the peaceable fruit of righteousness unto them which are exercised thereby." (Heb 12:11). "Follow peace with all men, and holiness, without which no man shall see the Lord" (Heb 12:14).

These are some of the things I chose to do, and they brought me from the place of moving in and out of the line to a steadfast faith in God, moving toward the victory in Jesus.

Chapter Nine

A JOURNEY THROUGH HEAVEN AND HELL

I dreamed that I went to Heaven and stood before Jesus. I didn't see any of the glories of Heaven; I just saw Jesus. It was a glorious experience to stand in front of God in Heaven. It appeared that we had a conversation. Standing there in His presence, He told me that I had to come back because it wasn't my time. He told me that He was going to send me back by way of hell. Jesus also told me that when I got back to the earth, He wanted me to tell people about my trip. He said, "When you tell them, they're not going to believe you."

I felt myself moving through a tunnel and knew when I got to the place of hell because it was the blackest darkness I'd ever seen. As I continued traveling through the tunnel, I eventually hit the ground, and it was a sunny day. I noticed that I had a black scroll in my hand that looked and felt like hardened ash. This was proof that He'd sent me through hell. When I told people about my experience, they said things like, "That's a nice story." Just like the Lord said, they didn't believe me. I also shared it with my Sunday school class, and they said, "Ah, that's a nice story," but they took it lightly.

After that experience, I went through many trials and tribulations. I saw the assignments that He sent me and allowed me to do and that I could be a blessing to many by being obedient to what the Spirit was saying to me. I was tremendously blessed. I thought about the Apostle Paul's experience in 2 Corinthians 12 when he said he was caught up into the third Heaven. My experience was different, but I'm thankful for it, and I still remember it. Personal experiences with God helped me to stay strong in the Lord and be mindful of maintaining my integrity.

STATEMENTS OF TRUTH

1. We should continue to walk in faith, even if we don't understand all of the mysteries that the Lord sends. I continued my walk with God by faith, and many things unfolded with instructions and assignments. We don't have to see everything that the Lord is doing, but when we trust Him and obey, that pleases the Lord and will cause Him to respond to us.

2. God will lead and guide you and show you things that He wants you to know and do. Be obedient to God's voice. When people don't believe you, God knows what He told you or showed you. Be faithful anyway, because your reward is with God alone.

Chapter Ten

THE FRUIT PICKING DREAM AND ITS LESSONS

I dreamed I was picking fruit in a big field and putting it in a big black trash bag. I came upon some pepper pods. As I picked them, I heard a voice say, "Don't put the peppers in the bag; put the peppers in your pocket." As I continued picking fruit in the field, I looked up and saw a green road sign that said 55 South.

STATEMENTS OF TRUTH

The Lord revealed that the big field represented the world where the Lord sends believers to work after we're saved. Acts 1:8 tells us that we will have the power to become witnesses for Jesus. The bag represented keeping the fruit safe. When I picked the peppers and the voice said, "Don't put the peppers in the bag; put the peppers in your pocket," God was showing me that people come with different characteristics, and some have high temperaments, but God loves them all. As we win souls, we must be discerning and not put troubling people and kind people together, as it can cause problems. God will allow the power He's given us to become witnesses for Him to bring souls into the Kingdom of God. Proverbs 11:30 says, "The fruit of the righteous is a tree of life; and he that winneth souls is wise."

I was born and raised in Tennessee. After the dream, I was called to speak at a few revivals in Memphis and I did a book signing in Bolivar. I don't know if those experiences were the fulfillment of my dream or not, but when we traveled home, we always traveled on 55 South on our route.

Chapter Eleven

THE BANQUET AND THE UNEXPECTED ENEMY

I dreamed that I was at a banquet and someone came from behind me and pulled my jacket off my shoulders. When I looked around to see who it was, it was a person who had become my enemy without cause. I believe the Lord was showing me that sometimes we think our enemies are gone, but in due time, God will show us that just because we don't see them, it doesn't mean they don't exist. So we have to be prayerful and watchful at all times.

STATEMENTS OF TRUTH

The Word of God teaches us that we should pray at all times. Luke 18:1 says, "That men ought always to pray, and not to faint." The Word of

God also teaches us, "Be sober, be vigilant; because your adversary the devil, as a roaring lion, walketh about, seeking whom he may devour" (1 Pet 5:8). The Lord loves us and He will protect us if we pay attention to our surroundings. We should seek Him in prayer, asking Him to give us wisdom, knowledge, and understanding on how to handle uncomfortable and negative situations. He said, He would never leave us or forsake us, He'll be right there. All we need to do is be in the right place with God, and He will always help us.

Chapter Twelve

THE MORTUARY DREAM AND THE CALL TO THE SPIRITUALLY DEAD

I dreamed I went to work in a mortuary. In my dream, I was walking to my job. When I got there, the area looked secluded. As I walked up to this huge building, I opened the door and walked down a large corridor that was much wider than a regular hallway. It was quite a distance from the entrance, so I began to wonder, "Where am I going?" I knew it was my job because I had my lunch with me. When I turned around, I was in the morgue, and this was my job. Hallelujah, help me Lord.

When I woke up, I asked the Lord what the dream meant, because my thinking process would never lead me to look for a job in a morgue. It didn't fit my job qualifications or desires for work, so I knew it wouldn't be a good fit for someone like me. The Lord told me at that point, that He had called me to work with people who are dead in trespasses and sin. Also, that through life, He would lead me to places guiding people to Salvation, showing them that healing and deliverance were for them.

STATEMENTS OF TRUTH

1. The Lord can send us on assignments that we have no desire to do. Remember, there are treasured and unfavorable places. There are people that need Jesus, and God has equipped His people to go and bring them out of dark places to safety.
2. We can't afford to be fearful. 2 Timothy 1:7 says, "For God hath not given us the spirit of fear; but of power, and of love, and of a sound mind."

Chapter Thirteen

A MOTHER'S PRAYER AND DIVINE PROTECTION

I dreamed that one of my sons was in an accident while playing basketball and was badly injured. I got out of bed and began to cry out to the Lord about it.

A few days later, I went to the store. When I returned, an ambulance was in my driveway, getting ready to take my son to the hospital for an injured arm from playing football. I was thankful to the Lord for covering him. I'm also thankful to the Lord for allowing me to be obedient and to get up and pray about the dream so that it wouldn't be a worse case.

STATEMENTS OF TRUTH

1. The dream showed me that my child was going to be in trouble. I got out of bed and began to call on the name of the Lord. The dream came to pass, and all I could do was thank the Lord for His protection.
2. When we pray, we must believe what we're praying about, whether we're praying about expected things or unexpected things.
3. We should not only pray for ourselves but for all people. Mark 11:24 says, "Therefore I say unto you, what things soever ye desire, when ye pray, believe that ye receive them, and ye shall have them."

Chapter Fourteen

THE LOVE TEST AND THE WAKE-UP CALL

I dreamed I missed the Rapture. It started with someone I thought I knew very well. Somewhere in the beginning of my life with the Lord, I experienced the worst level of offense that I had ever experienced, and I couldn't let it go. The person who caused the offense just wanted to go back to business as usual without saying "I'm sorry." I don't know what I was thinking, as I was very young in the Lord as well. But I was severely stiff about it and kept holding onto it until one morning, about 4:00 a.m., I dreamed that I missed the Rapture.

In the dream, I told myself I did not miss the Rapture because I knew that I lived right and always tried to please God. But although these were my personal thoughts, I saw people in the dream running, screaming, and hollering because they had been left behind. They should have been saved but were left behind because some things in their lives weren't right. I was still in denial and kept telling myself it wasn't the Rapture of the Church because I was still here. To test the facts, I went to my friend's job during lunchtime and asked someone if they had seen her. They said, "Yeah, she was sitting over there on that bench," but she wasn't there, only her lunch was.

In deep disappointment, I couldn't believe it. I felt like a child being corrected harshly by a parent and strongly insisting, "But I didn't do anything." Then I woke up, and the room was pitch black. As I lay there, it seemed that the dream experience was real. As I thought on it, my memory was refreshed by the Holy Spirit. He brought the incident to my mind that I was holding onto and how I allowed it to put me in a low state. I immediately repented to God and to the person. Yes, sometimes you also need to repent to the ones involved to free yourself. It's been many years since then, but I've never found myself in that predicament again.

STATEMENTS OF TRUTH

1. Don't allow yourself to get distracted by tests and trials.
2. "Pray without ceasing" (1 Thess 5:17).
3. Always be quick to forgive (Matt 6:14–15).
4. Meditate on His Word continually (John 8:31–32).
5. Continue to live right, do right, and be right at all times.
6. The Lord will come at a time when people are not aware, and we must be ready when He returns for us. These are things that we must remember so we will be ready when the Lord returns for His people:
   - God is love, and we must become what God is (1 John 4:16).
   - God is love, and He is fair.

- This incident happened when I was very young in the Lord. But being young is no excuse for not overcoming an offense. We must learn how to forgive people who hurt us. If we don't forgive, neither will we be forgiven (Matt 6:14–15).
- Sometimes people focus on the guilty parties, but God is looking at how you respond to a situation.
- When conflict arises, the best thing to do is remember the Word of God and what Jesus would have you to do.
- There are a lot of people today holding grudges, being mean, hateful, and bitter. I've met a lot of them, and we all know some of them. These people act like they don't understand what the Word of God is saying. I thank God for allowing me to have that experience. Know this, someone will always be doing or saying something to hurt you or pick on you. Keep your place in God. If it's something that the person did or said, you don't have to retaliate, because the Lord said vengeance belongs to Him (Rom 12:19).
- We can't afford to let anything or anyone cause us to miss the Lord.
- The Lord is coming back for His people, and we have to be in a state of readiness (1 Thess 4:16). Matthew 24:44 says, "Therefore be ye also ready: for in such an hour as ye think not the Son of Man cometh." We need to make that change from walking with an old attitude. Ephesians 4:21–32 shows believers how they ought to be and what we need to lay aside and put on spiritually to be ready when the Lord comes back for us. Matthew 24:48–51 says, "But and if that evil servant shall say in his heart, My lord delayeth his coming; And he shall begin to smite his fellowservants

and to eat and drink with the drunken; The lord of that servant shall come in a day when he looketh not for him, and in an hour that he is not aware of, And shall cut him asunder, and appoint him his portion with the hypocrites: there shall be weeping and gnashing of teeth."

- Always pray that the Lord will bless you and pray for deliverance from the negativity in your own spirit. If we keep it inside, sooner or later, it will cause us to explode, and the people who witness it will say, "I'm so disappointed because she or he did that." The evil servant was an example of this.
- We need to ask the Lord to help us become who He is in spirit and in truth.

Chapter Fifteen

THE END-OF-LIFE BRIDGE

I dreamed my husband and I were crawling across a narrow bridge, and it felt very scary to me. It appeared to be covered with leather and felt like a couch in texture. It felt like if I didn't move carefully, I could fall off. As we continued to move across the narrow bridge, I slid and fell to the ground while my husband went on across it alone.

STATEMENTS OF TRUTH

The Lord was showing me that I had gone with my husband as far as I could go. Not long after that, he transitioned home to be with the Lord. In his last days, he left evidence that he was with Jesus. There are many struggles in life, and it's important to press on in your walk with the Lord and continue in righteousness. Matthew 24:13 says, "But he that shall endure unto the end, the same shall be saved."

Chapter Sixteen

THE DREAM OF THE MOB
AND DIVINE GUIDANCE

I was working as a night caregiver. My client was asleep for the night. As I stayed through my shift, I slipped into a dream. I dreamed a mob of people was coming for me. I heard a big commotion outside. I went to the window and looked out to see what it was. The mob of people had lit torches. It was a horrifying experience.

I woke up and began to think about the dream. I said to myself, "I've never done anything to deserve anyone hunting me down like this." I came to the conclusion that my time was up on this job and that God was leading me to go home until He gave me another job.

I put in my two-week notice. I felt like I didn't want to stick around and wait to see what was going to happen; I wanted to move quickly, because I am a prophetic dreamer. My dreams came to pass even before I knew the Lord. But since I knew the Lord and had received that message in my dream, I knew I had to get out before the trouble came. Trouble did come, but I wasn't a part of it. I thank God for covering me again.

STATEMENTS OF TRUTH

1. You don't have to be a prophet for the Lord to show you things to come. If you have been born again, it means that His Spirit abides in you and He will show you His purpose and what you need to know.

2. It doesn't matter how many enemies you have; remember and know that God's got you. Meditate on the Word of God. Psalm 27:1–3 says, "The Lord is my light and my salvation; whom shall I fear? The Lord is the strength of my life; of whom shall I be afraid? When the wicked, even mine enemies and my foes, came upon me to eat up my flesh, they stumbled and fell. Though an host should encamp against me, my heart shall not fear: though war should rise against me, in this will I be confident."

Chapter Seventeen

HEALED FROM DIABETES

Years ago, I dreamed that I saw someone walk through my house, pick up my blood sugar testing machine, and walk out the front door with it. When I woke up and thought on it, I believed that at some point in my life, God was going to heal me of type 2 diabetes.

Three or four months later, I noticed my blood sugar numbers were coming down to a normal range, like 120–130. My A1C always stayed around seven. When I went to the doctor for my check-up a few months ago, my A1C had gone up to eight, possibly from the stress of being a caregiver and watching negative things happen that I couldn't do anything about. It wasn't from a bad eating plan, because I stayed on track with eating right. I told myself that I had to be intentional about working on my health, after that my A1C went back down to seven.

I will continue to walk out my healing through faith according to what the Lord showed me in the dream. I believe it because the Lord completes His work. Concerning diabetes, I know that eating right and staying active are very important. If we do these things, God can heal us as we pray and believe it. He puts things in our minds so that we can work together with Him.

STATEMENTS OF TRUTH

1. I am a prophetic dreamer. Most of my dreams come to pass. Sometimes God will show me in dreams what He will do and how He will move.
2. When you are a child of God, He will move for you. Proverbs 3:5–6 says, "Trust in the Lord with all thine heart; and lean not unto thine own understanding. In all thy ways acknowledge him, and he shall direct thy paths."
3. Although our gifts that the Lord imparts to us may be different, when we use what He's given us, it all works together for His glory. There is "no respect of persons with God" (Rom 2:11). The truth is what the Lord does for one He'll do for another righteous person.

Chapter Eighteen

THE JOB OPPORTUNITY

In the early '70s, another incident happened when my oldest son was a toddler. I was walking in the area where we lived at the time, and I saw a business that I thought would be a good place to work. I told myself that I would come back and apply for a job there soon. One day, I laid down to take a nap, and I was awakened by a voice saying, "If you go to that place and apply for a job, they will hire you." I went to the place, and they hired me on the spot.

Because of my own personal experiences with the Lord before and after Salvation, I don't doubt anyone who says they have heard from God. There will come a time when all of us will need someone to hear our truths. Romans 8:30–31 says, "Moreover whom he did predestinate, them he also called: and whom he called, them he also justified: and whom he justified, them he also glorified. What shall we then say to these things? If God be for us, who can be against us?"

STATEMENTS OF TRUTH

1. The Lord will always do something in our lives to show that He exists and is real to us.
2. My experience was showing me that I could trust in God and He was getting my attention.
3. We're on God's mind even before we knew Him; He has a plan that one day we will be saved.

PART TWO

DEMONIC EXPERIENCES

Chapter One

A DEMONIC ENCOUNTER AT LUNCH

One of my friends introduced me to a lady who wanted to connect with me in the ministry. She invited me to lunch. We were having a regular conversation while sitting at the table waiting to be served, when suddenly I heard a growl. I asked her if she said something, and she told me in a growl that she knew who I was. In the same growling voice, she told me that I was a powerful woman of God. I tell you the truth, I was ready to leave there without lunch. That experience took away my appetite. After she growled and that spirit spoke out of her, she returned to her normal voice. I could tell that she wasn't aware of what had just happened.

It's amazing that demons know the people of God while some people don't care to know you at all.

STATEMENTS OF TRUTH

1. Don't waver in your faith when unexpected things show up. There's something to learn; wait for it.
2. If you are a born-again believer, by the Word of God, God knows who you are. He knows your name.
3. There is no respecter of persons with the Lord (Rom 2:11), although assignments may differ.
4. The devil knows who you are as well. If he gets a chance, he'll show up and tell you.

Acts 19:11–17 speaks of the seven sons of Sceva. They observed what they saw Paul do by the hand of God "so that from his body were brought unto the sick handkerchiefs or aprons, and the diseases departed from them, and the evil spirits went out of them." The seven sons of Sceva attempted to mimic the power of God as Paul did. We read in verse 13 that they "took upon them to call over them which had evil spirits the name of the Lord Jesus, saying, We adjure you by Jesus whom Paul preacheth." Verses 15–16 state, "And the evil spirit answered and said, 'Jesus I know, and Paul I know; but who are ye?' And the man in whom the evil spirit was leaped on them, and overcame them, and prevailed against them, so that they fled out of that house naked and wounded." They did not have the Spirit of God, so they didn't know Jesus. When they attempted to cast out the spirits, the evil spirit spoke out of the man and said, "I know Jesus, I know Paul, but who are you?" This proves that the devil knows true believers. Casting out devils is one of the signs that will follow those who believe (Mark 16:15).

Chapter Two

A DEMONIC ENCOUNTER WITH A TROUBLED MAN

I was at church in my office when a young man came and knocked on the door. He asked if I had time to talk to him, and I said sure. He immediately told me that there was a spirit inside of him and he wanted to be free of it. Over the years, he had regularly been tormented by spirits, and although he had been delivered, he kept going back to the places where he picked up the spirits. On the previous occasions, I always had someone with me when praying over him. Each time he received prayer, he was delivered because he wanted to be free. After receiving prayer, he would say thank you and that he felt free again.

I looked up at him, and he seemed troubled.

I asked, "What is it?" and he didn't answer.

As I spoke stronger to him, he responded and said, "They're talking to me. They're telling me to jump on her."

His troubled look showed that he didn't want to do what they were telling him to do, so I continued the prayer of deliverance until he knew that he was free of the spirits and they were trying to control him from the outside of his body. No matter how long you've worked with certain things, God can always increase your knowledge and experience. If you know someone who has this condition, don't pray with them alone. The Lord may not always let someone tell you that they have that kind of problem for a reason, like the example of the woman who started growling while talking. There's nothing to be afraid of as these kinds of examples are in the Bible. If you are ever in a situation like that and you know the Lord, remember what the Scriptures say about the signs that follow believers (Mark 16:17). The Lord gives His people different experiences and encounters, and these are my experiences that the Lord gave to me to share with the readers.

STATEMENTS OF TRUTH

1. We don't know who carries evil spirits except when the Lord reveals it or the person tells us.
2. When you're in this type of situation, as much as possible, try to have strong believers around you to help pray for the individual's deliverance.
3. If the truth be told, not all believers want to deal with this part of the ministry. I remember years ago a situation arose with someone who had an evil spirit, and the people who were there to help started backing up. The qualifications for any type of spiritual experiences are found in Matthew 22:37–40. Jesus said, "Thou shalt love the

Lord thy God with all thy heart, and with all thy soul, and with all thy mind. This is the first and great commandment. And the second is like unto it, Thou shalt love thy neighbor as thyself." If we don't love the Lord God and people the way He told us to, we will not be helping others get delivered.

4. Mark 16:17 says, "These signs shall follow them that believe; In my name, they shall cast out devils."

5. It's no guarantee that someone will always be with you, but don't be afraid. Years ago a brother was shopping with his wife, and as she was trying on clothes, he was sitting in a chair waiting. A woman with an evil spirit moved toward him, growling. He had never seen anything like that before in his life, and he didn't know what to do. Because he was saved and filled with the Holy Ghost, he started saying, "Satan, the Lord rebuke you, I plead the blood of Jesus against you," until the woman turned and walked away. Somebody might say, "If that was me, I would have cast the spirit out of her." But every situation is different, and not everyone with an evil spirit is seeking deliverance. In these situations, don't forget that you've been filled with the Holy Spirit; He will guide you and tell you what to do.

6. The only protection we all have from evil spirits is to walk in obedience to the Word of God. That's where the true power of God is. If you don't walk and live in obedience to the Word of God, when a demonic situation shows up and your life doesn't fit the situation, just get out of the way and move to safety. Ask God to heal and deliver you so that you'll be ready next time to help.

Chapter Three

THE WILD WOMAN AND DELIVERANCE AT CHURCH

Years ago, we were about to have Sunday School when someone called and said she was bringing a woman to church. She stated that the woman was acting really wild and was making her lose control of the car. The woman's spirit was so wild that she had a hard time getting her out of the car and into the church. As she came to the door with the woman, she continued to scream and try to fight. She was ministered to and prayed for, and she calmed down and was delivered.

STATEMENTS OF TRUTH

1. Believers have been given the power to witness to those who don't know Christ. Acts 1:8 says, "But ye shall receive power, after that the Holy Ghost is come upon you: and ye shall be witnesses unto me both in Jerusalem, and in all Judaea, and in Samaria, and unto the uttermost part of the earth."
2. Mark 16:17 says, "And these signs shall follow them that believe; in my name shall they cast out devils."

Chapter Four

THE BLOOD-COVERED MAN AND THE CALL TO DELIVERANCE

A man came to the church and asked for prayer. When the prayer began, he started rolling his eyes back, and his teeth were covered with blood. He began to act wild. At that time, he didn't seek deliverance and stayed in that state. I pray wherever he is today, if he's still alive, that he has been freed from that torment.

STATEMENTS OF TRUTH

1. John 14:6 says, "Jesus saith unto him, I am the way, the truth, and the life: no man cometh unto the Father, but by me."

2. Every spiritual blessing that we need must come through Jesus Christ, whether it's salvation, healing, or deliverance. In John 15:5, Jesus says, "For without me ye can do nothing."

3. We must take all of our troubles to the Lord and ask Him to help us. In the days that Jesus was on earth, all who came to Him were healed, delivered, and set free from every infirmity they had. He would do the same today if we would ask Him (Matt 4:23–25).

4. Malachi 3:6 says, "For I am the Lord, I change not."

Chapter Five

THE SPIRIT THAT REFUSED TO LEAVE

A spirit refused to come out of an individual. I walked into the back room of the church where a crowd of people had gathered around a young lady. As I drew closer to see what was going on, I saw that the young lady was out of control and her eyes were rolled back. I stepped in closer to pray for her deliverance. It appeared that some force was trying to break her neck. I began to pray for her, commanding the spirit to loose her and let her go. When nothing happened, I backed away and began to talk to God. I prayed and asked God what was happening. I examined my own life as to why the spirit wasn't releasing her, because this was the first time that had ever happened.

Next, my husband walked through and asked what was going on. I said, "She has a spirit in her and it won't let her go."

His reply was, "If she hadn't attacked that person, she wouldn't be in that situation."

I realized that no one could help her because she needed to repent.

STATEMENTS OF TRUTH

1. We can't be mean and cruel toward others, no matter the reason, and expect to have the same loving relationship with a loving God. It's just not so because the Word of God shows us that God cannot and will not connect Himself with evil. Romans 6:1–2 asks, after we are born again, "What shall we say then? Shall we continue in sin, that grace may abound? God forbid. How shall we, that are dead to sin, live any longer therein?"

2. The Lord expects us to continue in His Word. John 8:31, Jesus said, "If ye continue in my word, then are ye my disciples indeed."

3. Once we start our life with Christ, there is no turning back. In Luke 9:62, Jesus said, "No man, having put his hand to the plough, and looking back, is fit for the kingdom of God."

PART THREE

LIFE EXPERIENCES

Chapter One

A PROPHET'S VISIT AND A DIVINE ENCOUNTER

A man of God who was a friend of one of my family members came and knocked on the door. As he entered the house, he greeted everyone. I didn't know him personally, but he began to talk to me and prophesied things that God was showing him about me.

The first thing he said was that as he walked up the driveway, "I saw you downstairs sewing and working on a sleeve." I listened because so far what he was saying was true. I was sewing right before he walked up. He continued to prophesy to me, saying, "Someone in here has an entrepreneur anointing." As he talked, I looked at him and smiled because the things he was calling out were regular things that I considered normal. He continued, "Someone in here has a lot of power." After that, he said,

"That's you. I want to pray for you because God is going to do great things for you and through you." As the man of God approached me to lay hands on me, the power of God knocked him back. It was like a strong wind pushed him back. He was determined to pray for me, but the next time he attempted to lay hands on me, he fell back again and slid across the floor. It was an experience that I will never forget—a prophetic experience.

John 18:6 says, "As soon then as he had said unto them, I am He, they went backward and fell to the ground." This is the only Scripture that reminded me of my experience. I am not Jesus, but I am a true daughter of His in the Gospel, and so are you if you're saved—you are His sons and daughters, and we boast only in the Lord.

I'll say this: don't ever let people put you down or try to make you think you're not important, because you are important to the Lord. So, when the Lord sends a strong personal word to you either face to face or by a person of God, we can accept it and not get prideful because God gave us an unusual experience.

I had never seen or experienced anything like this before. Even though it happened in the presence of witnesses, I never felt led to share it because I didn't think anyone would believe it. The man of God stated that God was going to do great things with me and through me. I believe that God chose me for this writing to help people who are struggling in their faith and to show them that they are important to the Lord. If that's you, let me remind you that He's got you. Everything He wills for you will come to pass, and all that He intends for you to know, you will know and obey.

Later on in life, a few years ago, a close friend of mine who operates in the prophetic told me, "Ruby, you don't know who you are in God." I asked her what she meant, and she said, "You have a lot of power from God." She continued to reiterate and repeat it. And I believed her, because I'd never shared that story with her or anyone else.

STATEMENTS OF TRUTH

1. The Lord knows how to prepare our hearts for future assignments.
2. Keep praying and believing until all that the Lord said toward you come to pass.

Chapter Two

MY LIFE'S DESIRE AFTER SALVATION

After I received Salvation, I just wanted to be with the Lord. I wasn't trying to be anybody special or be anybody's minister. But in due season, as I continued to be obedient to the Word of God, I was called by Him to minister Salvation to the lost and to teach healing and deliverance to the people of God, just as He had healed me. I wanted to let the world know that our relationship with the Lord is for keeps, because God Himself has given us the gift of life—eternal life.

After I got saved, I was excited to have a new life in Christ Jesus. My only desire with this new life was to please the Lord with my whole being. I understood that God does not tolerate sin, so if I did or said anything from my old self, I repented and asked God to help me avoid making the same mistakes again. It was special to me to know that God chooses His people for His purpose and glory, and I was glad to be one of the chosen.

The most difficult part of my Salvation experience was learning how to pass tests and trials. For example, I had to learn not to rebel against God and to not render evil for evil when I was mistreated. I learned to study how Jesus handled negative situations, and I relied on Scriptures like Romans 8:28, which says, "And we know that all things work together for good to them that love God, to them who are the called according to his purpose."

When people see us, we don't know what our lives look like to them. I found out that even though we love God with all of our might, we are not exempt from suffering in this life. So, every now and then, God will send a prophet or prophetess to speak into our lives to encourage us on up the road.

STATEMENTS OF TRUTH

1. Men and women with prophetic gifts will show up to encourage the people of God when they need it.
2. Prophets will show up when you least expect it.
3. They come to bring you hope for your future, especially when you feel hopeless.
4. They will confirm things that you already knew.
5. They can tell you things that you don't know by revealing what God is showing them that will come to pass in your life.

Accept the people that God sends to you because they have been sent to help you get to the place in God you should be. Remember this, it's His purpose, not yours.

Chapter Three

PROPHETIC WORDS FROM MY PASTOR

In the '80s, God sent me on jobs for certain people. My pastor at the time would tell me that I wasn't supposed to work a natural job because I was meant to work for the Lord. Then he would chuckle and say, "You can get a job if you want to, but something will happen and you'll have to leave." And as I proceeded here and there to get jobs, as surely as the pastor spoke, I would go to my jobs to work, something would happen, and I would have to leave.

But I always noticed that right before I left, I made friends with different people, and the Lord would call one of their names and say, "This is the one I sent you here for." There were about five instances where I went to work and God spoke to me and said, "I sent you here for this person." Many times, other people were connected to the people whose names God called for me to speak the Word of the Lord to, and they all either received Christ or came closer to Jesus and continued to walk with Him.

At one of my jobs, I was bringing a coworker storybook tracts on the life of Christ for her to take home. One day, she said to me, "Ruby, you know those little books that you've been giving me?" I said yes, and she said, "I didn't read them, but my boyfriend is reading them."

One day, our church sponsored a movie called *The Rapture*. I called my friend from work to invite her to go. Her boyfriend answered the phone, and I introduced myself to him. Since he answered the phone, I invited him to come. To my surprise, he said, "I would love to come."

That night, the church was packed full of people. The movie played, and afterward, the minister made the altar call with prayer. I didn't want to turn around and look behind me because I didn't know what the man looked like. Suddenly, I heard a voice from behind me say, "Let me get up and go up here." The man stepped into the aisle, went to the altar, received Jesus, and went on his way praising God. He continued to learn about Jesus and became a great soul winner.

He owned a van back then. The Sunday after his conversion, he missed Sunday School, and I began to get concerned that he had gone back from the Lord. But in the middle of the service, he came down the middle aisle with countless people who had come with him to the church. Many of them were saved and baptized according to the Word of God in Acts 2:38. They stayed with the Lord until this day, and some of them have gone home to be with the Lord.

What I know and understand is that all of us have a story to tell about Jesus. Our experiences may be different, but we should share our story, because God has given us the power to witness and to deliver our messages or stories. Isaiah 55:11 says, "So shall my word be that goeth forth out of my mouth. It shall not return unto me void, but it shall accomplish that which I please, and it shall prosper in the thing whereto I sent it." Remember, God has given us all some gifts and talents. If it's only but one, He wants us to recognize what He's given us, step out, be obedient, and do the works. He will be right there to help you do whatever it is. A good example is the parable of the talents that Jesus spoke of in Matthew 25:14–30. God has given us gifts to multiply in the Kingdom of God. We must be about our Father's business so that He may say unto us, "Well done, thou good and faithful servant, enter thou into the joy of the Lord."

STATEMENTS OF TRUTH

1. As we live for the Lord, He will continue to help us and train us in the way we should go.
2. Sometimes He'll send people who are already skilled to help us on our way as we work for the Lord.
3. As we honor the Lord in our work, the manifestations of the Lord will appear, and God will be glorified.

Chapter Four

THE POWER OF TOUCHING AND AGREEING

One summer day in 1979, when I had known the Lord for over a year, we were leaving the church, and everyone was going to their cars. I started to cross the street when another sister caught up with me and said, "Don't worry Sister Harvey, Brother Harvey is coming on in."

I said, "I do believe that," and then a thought came to my mind: "This year, this year," and I said to the sister, "And it will happen this year." As the sister started to walk away, I stopped her and said, "Let's touch and agree according to the Word of God that he will come to Christ this year." I believed the Word of God was true and wanted to act upon it. The Scripture says in Matthew 18:19–20, "Again I say unto you, that if two of you shall agree on earth as touching anything that they shall ask, it shall be done for them of my Father which is in Heaven. For where two or three are gathered together in my name, there am I in the midst of them."

From August to November, nothing happened. The month of December came, and nothing happened through the whole month. On the night of December 31st, I went to choir rehearsal. The church was in a three-day shut-in and our end-of-the-year fast. My husband came at the end of the choir rehearsal to pick me up, and he sat in the back. My pastor's wife was over the shut-in service, and she asked my husband to come a little closer to the front, and he said, "I'm all right here." She wouldn't give up on him and asked him again. He got up and went down to the altar and stood there in front of her. As she instructed and ministered to him, he closed his eyes and began to praise God. His spirit was broken, and he was filled with the Holy Ghost at the altar and later submitted himself to baptism according to the Scripture in Acts 2:38.

STATEMENTS OF TRUTH

The Word of God is powerful, and if we live what it says, it will be manifested in our lives. When it looked like it wasn't going to happen, on the last day of the year, God answered that agreement. Try not to doubt when you've touched and agreed about a situation. Be still and let the Word of God work for you. Isaiah 55:11 says, "So shall my word be that goeth forth out of my mouth: it shall not return unto me void, but it shall accomplish that which I please, and it shall prosper in the thing whereto I sent it." And this is what the Lord said.

Chapter Five

THE POWER OF A CRAZY PRAISE

I was visiting a church service when the preacher stopped in the middle of his message and said, "Some of you need God to do some special things, and if that's you, I want you to get out of your seat without thinking about it and give God a crazy praise." People began to run to the altar, giving God a crazy praise. I don't know what my praise looked like, but it felt wild and crazy and ugly.

Not very long after that, we had a prophet preaching at our church, and my son came to the altar. The Spirit of God fell on him, and he was saved and filled with the Holy Ghost. He is still saved today, and that was over a decade ago. Sometimes you have to challenge your faith to do more and step out publicly and do something unusual for you. According to your faith, God will prove Himself to you.

STATEMENTS OF TRUTH

1. Sometimes to receive something you never had you have to do something you never did. James 2:17–18 says, "Even so faith, if it hath not works, is dead, being alone. Yea, a man may say, Thou hast faith, and I have works: shew me thy faith without thy works, and I will shew thee my faith by my works." Both call for actions. There will come a time in our lives when we will just have to move out and do something to show our faith in God.

2. After the woman with the issue of blood had spent all of her living on physicians and couldn't be healed by any, she went to Jesus. Her faith caused her to reach out and touch the hem of His garment. Immediately she was healed, and "Jesus said, Somebody hath touched me: for I perceive that virtue is gone out of me." The woman was afraid, and He said to her, "Daughter, be of good comfort: thy faith hath made thee whole; go in peace" (Luke 8:43–48).

3. Deliverance can sometimes take a long time when we don't move out in faith. The Scripture states in John 5 that a certain man had an infirmity for thirty-eight years. When Jesus saw him lying there and knew that he had been in that condition for a long time, He said to him, "Wilt thou be made whole?"

   The man answered, "Sir, I have no man, when the water is troubled, to put me into the pool: but while I am coming, another steppeth down before me."

   Jesus said to him, "Rise, take up thy bed, and walk."

Immediately the man was made whole, took up his bed, and walked (John 5:5–9).

4. Some of us are just like the impotent man. When Jesus asked him if he wanted to be made whole, instead of saying, "Yes, Lord," he began to make excuses about why he had been in that condition for thirty-eight years. The Lord paid no attention to his excuses. He just told the man to rise, take up his bed, and walk. We must practice stepping out by faith to receive our blessings. It may consist of saying something or doing something. Faith is the only thing that moves the Lord. Faith and works are the power that activates a move of God.

Chapter Six

MIRACLE OF A DECEASED MAN

One day I was fasting, and someone called me and said, "Can you come over here? Someone has passed away." I felt a little strange going, because I'd never been called to an assignment like that before. When I got there, the coroner was there to pick up the body. Before his passing, I had been having Bible classes with the person. As I walked closer to the body as they were zipping him up, I started asking the family members questions such as, "What happened?" As soon as I spoke, the bag moved, and a voice spoke from inside the bag. They unzipped the bag to free the person, because the individual was no longer deceased. He lived a few years longer.

STATEMENTS OF TRUTH

The Word of God states in John 14:12 the Lord said, "Verily, verily, I say unto you, He that believeth on me, the works that I do shall he do also; and greater works than these shall he do; because I go unto my Father." Romans 8:11 states, "But if the Spirit of him that raised up Jesus from the dead dwell in you, he that raised up Christ from the dead shall also quicken your mortal bodies by his Spirit that dwelleth in you." The Lord never tells us all of His plans, but enough for us to trust Him. As He had led me to fast, I had no idea that it would take me to a situation like that. I felt so humbled that the Lord trusted me enough to send me on that mission. And through that miracle, God was glorified. When it's time to move, don't question God. Just move out by faith and watch Him move.

Chapter Seven

OPEN VISION OF SOMEONE FALLING FROM A DARK PLACE

About two decades ago, some children were playing a game and having a great time, laughing and enjoying themselves. Suddenly, one of the children turned a pale gray color in the face and had a terrified expression. It looked so scary that I could barely get my voice up enough to ask, "What is it?"

The child couldn't speak at first, but then said, "I saw someone falling in a bottomless place. It was really dark." The child then called a name.

My legs felt like rubber; the vision took my strength away. The child also stated that the person had on white clothes, but they had smudges of black spots all over them, and the person looked tormented.

STATEMENTS OF TRUTH

1. The experience was very spooky. The disturbing thing about the incident was that the child recognized who it was. The person had passed away some years before.
2. Sometimes when we hear of things of this sort, we may want to dissect it and reason about it. But when you experience it personally, it's different.
3. Fear has torment, and God has not given us a spirit of fear.
4. This experience caused me to hold on to Jesus tighter, remembering the things that He said in the Word of God, such as in Matthew 22:37–40: to love God with all my heart and with all my soul and with all my mind and to love my neighbor as myself.
5. Love your enemies.
6. Forgive others.
7. Show your love for the Lord by keeping His commandments.
8. Remember, just because we understand what God is saying in the Word of God, everyone doesn't understand. God sends His people to help others in whatever way He chooses.

Chapter Eight

DIVINE INTERVENTION AGAINST WORKPLACE BULLYING

About a decade ago, there was a woman who was picked on every day when she came to work. Every day, the bully would do something to humiliate her in front of the other workers. One day, the bully took the bullying a step further and lifted her arms in the air to hit the woman, but her arms locked in the air with pain. The bully screamed and had a lot of negative things to say, but she never bothered the woman again.

STATEMENTS OF TRUTH

1. If you're bullied, try not to render evil for evil. "See that none render evil for evil unto any man; but ever follow that which is good, both among yourselves and to all men" (1 Thess 5:15).

2. We should never have an attitude to rebel first. "If it be possible, as much as lieth in you, live peaceably with all men. Dearly beloved, avenge not yourselves, but rather give place unto wrath: for it is written, Vengeance is mine; I will repay, saith the Lord" (Rom 12:18–19).

3. In obeying the Scriptures, you're in a safe place with the Lord. Operating otherwise draws negative consequences. "Whoso diggeth a pit shall fall therein: and he that rolleth a stone, it will return upon him. A lying tongue hateth those that are afflicted by it" (Prov 26:27–28a).

Chapter Nine

FAITH IN THE FACE OF ADVERSITY

My husband and I started a ministry in the basement of our home on January 1, 1986. We were bringing in children from the neighborhood and teaching them the Word of God. The ministry was soon named Bethlehem Church of God. I was busy doing different things for the ministry and working for the Lord, and members were continually added to the church.

On February 3, 1986, I had a dental appointment. As I started to get ready, I heard a voice speak to me and say, "You don't have to go today." I stopped to think about it and went to the calendar to check the date. I said to myself, "But I do have to go." My baby girl was five years old at that time, and I was taking her with me.

As we prepared to leave, I got to the car and it was raining. I put my hand on the door and it felt like some type of evil force shoved me to the ground. I don't know if my foot slipped, but I was under the car on my back, and my pelvic bone felt broken. My left arm was limp, and I was hemorrhaging really badly from my arm. I told my baby to go and knock on the door and tell her dad that I was hurt and couldn't move. My baby responded, "Mommy, I can't leave you, you are hurt." Keep in mind, she was five years old.

I laid under the car and prayed. "Lord, help me move my body or else I'll die right here." I began to push backward until I was up and able to walk to the door. Blood was pouring out of my arm so fast it could fill up a cup. The ambulance came and took me to the hospital. I had a compound fracture in my left arm. My arm broke like a stick, and the bone pierced my outer skin. The surgeon came and looked at my injury and said he couldn't touch it for twelve days because the bone pierced the skin. It could set up gangrene poisoning and I could lose my arm. After twelve days, the surgeon was able to complete the surgery with success. They took me to the recovery room and the feeling was coming back to my arm. It felt like someone had taken a hammer and beat my arm. They had put clamps and pins in the bones in my arm to hold it together, and after a year they would go back into the arm to remove the clamps and pins.

I was praying and talking to God, trying to understand it all. I was also talking to myself, looking for answers. My children came to visit me in the hospital. One of them, who was ten years old at the time and whom the Lord allowed to know my thoughts, said, "The devil has been talking to you and he told you that God doesn't love you. If God loved you, He wouldn't have let this happen to you." It sounded like the situation with

Job. If my life was in any way in error and I knew it, I would have to write that part as well. To my knowledge, there was no sin in my life that I was overlooking. As I went through all of the pain and misery, I had to listen to a few sideline observers speaking negatively. After I was healed, God did many great things in my life. Some of them are written in this book.

STATEMENTS OF TRUTH

1. Romans 8:28 tells us, "And we know that all things work together for good to them that love God, to them who are the called according to his purpose."
2. If your life pleases God, the devil will come for you. Remember, Joseph was hated by his brothers, and they put him in a pit. The devil wanted to destroy Joseph because God loved him and protected him. Haman wanted to destroy the Jews because he hated them. When people hate you, they don't want you to prosper, as the Word of God teaches us.
3. 1 Peter 5:8 says, "Be sober, be vigilant; because your adversary the devil, as a roaring lion, walketh about, seeking whom he may devour."
4. Jesus says in John 14:6a, "I am the way, the truth, and the life." When you have Jesus, you have everything you need, and you will not die before your time.
5. Sometimes we will meet with the unexpected. You won't always know the day, the hour, or the reason for the outcome. When you belong to God, He has a plan for your life. When the negative shows up, it's only a test. You have to be still and wait on God, knowing that He's coming to help you and He already knows what He will do.

6. There are some things that we are destined to go through. God does not cause these things, but He allows them to bring us to His purpose. Don't let the naysayers discourage you, because they don't know God's plan for you.

Chapter Ten

THE HARMFUL POWER OF LIES

Decades ago, I was sitting and talking with someone, having a general conversation. We only talked about the things this person shared about their life. I found out sometimes later, that this person told another individual, someone I knew but not personally, that I had talked about her really badly. That was far from the truth. That individual's name never came up at all. The individual who heard the lies came and told me what was said, and I told her those things weren't true at all and that her name never came up. It was discovered that this person I had talked with, did these types of things everywhere they went, targeting people with this game.

I began to wonder, why a person you hardly know would lie about you on purpose? The one who told the lies came back into our midst, laughing and talking as if she'd never done anything wrong. On two other occasions, I experienced the same thing with two other people. The first one stated that she knew people who could harm anyone who harmed them. She could make a call, and they could come and run over someone with their car. They could do a drive-by or whatever just because someone did them wrong.

This was certainly a test of my faith. Anyone who knows me, know I've never operated like that. The best way to protect yourself from this type of behavior is to try your best to go out with people that you know and who knows you.

STATEMENTS OF TRUTH

1. No one can benefit from lying. The first lie was told in Genesis 3:4 when the serpent said to the woman, "Ye shall not surely die."
2. Proverbs 6:16–17 says, "These six things doth the Lord hate: yea, seven are an abomination unto him: A proud look, a lying tongue, and hands that shed innocent blood."
3. Proverbs 12:22 says, "Lying lips are an abomination to the Lord, but they that deal truly are his delight."
4. Proverbs 19:5, 9 says, "A false witness shall not go unpunished, and he that speaketh lies shall not escape." "He that speaketh lies shall perish."
5. Acts 5:1–11 recounts how Ananias and his wife Sapphira fell dead after lying to the Holy Ghost.

6. Psalm 34:14 encourages us to "depart from evil and do good; seek peace and pursue it."

7. At the end of every offense, we must be willing to forgive to the point where we're not rehearsing what happened over and over again in our minds. When things seem hard to conquer, we shouldn't pretend that it's gone away. Instead, we should go back to the Lord and ask Him to help us overcome it, because the Lord is coming back for overcomers. We can't afford to take chances missing the Lord when He returns.

8. If an offense becomes a stronghold in our lives, we must remember Matthew 6:14–15, where Jesus says, "For if you forgive men their trespasses, your heavenly Father will also forgive you. But if ye forgive not men their trespasses, neither will your Father forgive your trespasses."

9. Forgiveness is necessary for our Salvation. We can't live like the foolish virgins in Matthew 25:1–13, acting like they had their lives together when they did not. When the Lord came back, they were lost and terrified. It was their problem, and it was their fault.

Chapter Eleven

AN UNEXPECTED ASSIGNMENT

I was invited to MC a service. When I arrived, the people were on their knees in prayer. I was invited to the pulpit, and as I knelt in prayer, I heard the Spirit say, "Get your Bible, turn to Psalm 27, and read all of it." I read it.

Then I heard the Spirit say, "Turn to Matthew 5:16 and read it." I read it.

Then the Spirit said to me, "Your subject is 'Let your light shine.' You're not the MC, you are the speaker."

After a few minutes, I glimpsed the pastor of the church come out of his office. Looking across the room, he walked over to me and said, "If my speaker doesn't show up, will you bring the Word of God?"

I immediately said, "Yes, sir, I will." What else could I say? The Lord chose me for that time.

STATEMENTS OF TRUTH

1. When you know the Lord God and have been faithful to Him, He knows what He can trust you with.
2. Those of you who operate in the prophetic, remember Amos 3:7: "Surely the Lord God will do nothing, but He revealeth His secret unto His servants the prophets." This shows us that the Lord has chosen to reveal His plans to us.
3. Other Scripture proof that God will prepare His people and show them beforehand what He will have them do can be found in Acts 10. Before Cornelius's conversion, "God showed him in a vision to send some of his men to Joppa and ask for Peter. He was told that Peter would tell them what they needed to do." But the Lord had to also prepare Peter for the Gentiles coming to visit him. Cornelius and his household needed Salvation. This meeting wouldn't have happened if the Lord hadn't given them both a vision about the meeting place, because at that time, Jews and Gentiles weren't mixing like that (Acts 10:8–48).
4. When the Lord leads us and speaks to us, as we understand it and are obedient to the Lord's assignments, His mission is accomplished.

Chapter Twelve

ENDURING PUBLIC CRITICISM

I had to speak on a platform with some other people. At the end, one of them went to the microphone and said, "Evangelist Harvey took everything I had to say." Then she proceeded to openly talk about my clothes. I didn't understand her behavior toward me; it appeared to be personal. I felt she could have told me what she wanted me to know in private, but it came across as cruel and mean. I concluded that whatever she felt about me, she wanted everyone in the room to know. It was definitely a day of picking on me, even though I didn't have on trashy clothes.

At another church service, the same person was there. I was asked to take the platform, and she didn't like it. She showed the people that she didn't like it by turning around and sneering at me up and down. When we left the church that night and I got in the car, I was so glad it was nighttime because I didn't know if my husband had seen the situation, and I didn't want him to see me crying and broken over it. He then made a statement to let me know that he had seen the incident. He said, "I don't know what kind of spirit some people have that makes them think some people shouldn't be a part of the things of God." I didn't know either, but I knew that it was hurtful.

At another service where I was to speak, right before I was about to be introduced, they asked another person to say something. Here we go again. The person stated, "We don't need another person to say another word; we've already heard enough people talking." I believe that if you have the Spirit of God, you should know what is the right thing to say or not say. If our lives don't match what the Word of God is saying, whether we're old or young, we need to go back to the altar, repent, and ask God for forgiveness before we end up in a place without the Lord. I pray that people who carry these types of spirits will be delivered, because some people would not be able to handle it and would stop walking with God because of this treatment. The Scriptures speaks of people having blood on their hands because of the things that they did or didn't do to the people of God.

STATEMENTS OF TRUTH

1. John 10:10 says, "The thief cometh not, but for to steal, and to kill, and to destroy. I am come that they might have life, and that they might have it more abundantly."

2. John 15:18–19 says, "If the world hate you, ye know that it hated me before it hated you. If ye were of the world, the world would love his own: but because you are not of the world, but I have chosen you out of the world, therefore the world hateth you."

3. Jesus has laws that will deliver people out of conflicts, such as (Matthew 18:15): "Moreover if thy brother shall trespass against thee, go and tell him his fault between thee and him alone: if he shall hear thee, thou hast gained thy brother." If we handle our conflicts God's way, the outcome will be good. The Word of God teaches us to go to the person who offended us and not everyone else.

4. These are spiritual attacks called character assassinations, negatively speaking hate talk about others. These spirits are not in God's true Church or the Body of Christ, but they can work themselves through the brick-and-mortar building.

5. All believers will suffer here and there. (2 Timothy 3:12) says, "Yea, and all that will live godly in Christ Jesus shall suffer persecution." But the righteous are not a part of those who persecute believers; we know how that feels.

Chapter Thirteen

DIVINE
FINANCIAL PROVISION

Not long after I came to the Lord, there was a debt that I needed to pay in the amount of $125.00. As I recall, I went downtown to take care of some business. When I came out of the building, there was a long white envelope on the ground. I heard in my spirit to pick it up and keep walking, and I did that. When I returned to the car and got in, I opened the envelope and all I could say was "Jesus, Jesus, Jesus." My husband, who did not know the Lord at the time but was aware of my need for $125.00 for this debt, asked what it was. I told him about how I came across the envelope, and inside it was a brand new $100 bill and a new $20 bill.

As I rejoiced in the car about it, my husband sat quietly until I finished my praise and then said, "Now I know you don't believe that God just dropped that money out of the sky for you to pick it up."

I got quiet to make sure I gave the right answer, then said to him, "God will do whatever you need Him to do if you believe it." And yes, I believed it, and there was no identification in the envelope, so I knew that God supplied my need.

STATEMENTS OF TRUTH

1. We should stop worrying about things that we can't fix. Just pray and believe. Matthew 19:26 says, "With men this is impossible; but with God all things are possible."

Chapter Fourteen

MIRACULOUS HEALING

There was a drive-by shooting. A young man I knew went to a liquor store to buy something. As he came out of the store, there was a drive-by shooting, and a fragment of the bullet went into his head. I was very concerned about him. I went to the hospital to visit him. He was unconscious, and the doctor said the fragment was in his brain. They did surgery on him but could not reach the fragment, so it was still in his brain. I was so burdened as if he were my own child. He played with my children in the neighborhood. I went to see him and asked his mother if I could pray for him, and she said yes.

At that time, I hadn't known the Lord that long, but I had a lot of faith. As I began to pray for him, I laid my hand on his head, and I felt a sensation like electricity come down my arm, through my hand, and into his head. I left that place in amazement at what happened. The only explanation was that it was the power of God. A few days went by, and I hadn't heard anything. I walked to their house and asked his mother how he was doing. She said he was doing good. The doctors had a new report. They x-rayed his head again and said the fragment of the bullet wasn't there. What the first x-ray showed wasn't showing on the second x-ray. I knew it was because God healed him.

STATEMENTS OF TRUTH

1. All things are possible with God (Mark 9:23b).
2. Jesus healed the sick and raised the dead. He can do it again if we trust Him.
3. The doctors couldn't get the fragment of the bullet from his brain, but after prayer, they x-rayed him a second time and no fragment was there. God did it for him. The young man left the hospital healed.

Chapter Fifteen

BLIND WOMAN'S EYES OPENED

When my daughters were young adults, there was a lady we all loved who was blind. I sought the Lord through fasting and prayer, believing that if we went to visit her, God would open her eyes. The girls also joined the fast. After the days of fasting had ended, we went to pray for her. As we entered her room, she heard us talking and called each of us by name. We sat and talked to her for a while, then I asked her if she minded if we prayed for her so that she would be able to see. She said, "You can pray."

After the prayer, she looked at her hand, then around the room. She pointed out my daughters and called their names because she could see them. The next thing she did was look toward the window and told us what color the curtains were. We rejoiced with her because of what God had just done—opening her eyes so she could see.

STATEMENTS OF TRUTH

1. Jesus healed all manner of sickness and disease. Even the blind eyes came open so they could see.
2. It doesn't matter what type of condition you have; God can heal us all, whether it's a physical, mental, or emotional condition.
3. Jesus came to save, heal, and deliver His people.

Chapter Sixteen

CUT BRAKE LINES, UNBROKEN FAITH

A few years ago, after attending an event, I went to my car to leave. The car was making some noises as I attempted to back up. When I touched the brakes, the brake pedal went all the way to the floor. My son came out to look at it and said, "You can't drive the car. I'll take it back using the back streets and take it to my house." He had a difficult time getting it to his house. My mechanic came and towed it to his shop. After checking it out to see why the car had suddenly stopped working, he called me from his shop and said, "You have some very serious enemies because someone cut your brake line." To prove it was done on purpose, he told me, "It's a clean, smooth cut."

STATEMENTS OF TRUTH

1. We do have enemies, some of whom we know and some we don't.

2. We should follow and practice what Jesus taught about how to treat our enemies. Luke 6:27–28 says, "But I say unto you which hear, Love your enemies, do good to them which hate you. Bless them that curse you, and pray for them which despitefully use you."

3. When we are obedient and do as the Lord has commanded us to do in His Word, He will take care of our enemies, seen or unseen. When Saul sought out to destroy the Christians, the Lord met him near Damascus. In Acts 9:3–5, we read, "Suddenly there shined round about him a light from heaven: And he fell to the earth, and heard a voice saying unto him, Saul, Saul, why persecutest thou me? And he said, Who art thou, Lord? And the Lord said, I am Jesus whom thou persecutest."

4. When people allow themselves to be enemies to believers, they are the enemies of Jesus, and no one will ever block Jesus from doing His will through His people. Ephesians 4:32 says, "And be ye kind one to another, tenderhearted, forgiving one another, even as God for Christ's sake hath forgiven you."

5. As we journey on through life, we learn to be kind to everyone we meet. When it's time to introduce people to Jesus, remember we can win more souls with honey (being nice) than with vinegar (being sour). Now that we are new creatures in Christ Jesus, we should practice following what's right at all times.

Chapter Seventeen

WHAT LOOKS LIKE FAILURE CAN TURN INTO VICTORY

I founded I Care About Myself Ministry (ICAM) on March 8, 1996. People came to our meetings every first and third Saturday for salvation, healing, and deliverance. The Lord met us there in a powerful way. In 2002, we planned a trip to the Holiday Inn in Jackson, Tennessee, for our first out-of-town conference in our outreach ministry. It was a memorable journey. We were all ready and excited about the trip. Some people came and parked their cars on the church lot and others were dropped off, and as we waited for our transportation, things started going wrong.

First, when the bus pulled onto the lot to pick us up, it was not the bus we ordered. It looked like a bus from the '50s, and we all looked at it in amazement. I thought, "I know there is another bus because this is not the bus we ordered and paid for," but this was the bus they had sent, and it was too late to make amends because the office was closed, so we had to deal with this mishap. No one among us acted out of character because of the situation, and that was a blessing.

Second, as the bus left the lot, it didn't sound good. The sound was actually connected to the way the bus looked. It was prayer time for me. Third, before we got halfway on our journey, it started raining really bad, and the rain turned into a storm. The driver could hardly see. Fourth, the rainwaters started coming into the bus, rolling under our feet. No one was saying a word; the only thing you could hear was the windshield wipers making noise on that old bus. Finally, we made it. We all got off the bus and checked in.

While planning this trip, I wrote down everything that was needed, such as a keyboard, a microphone, speakers, etc. One of my children, who was twenty-one at the time, asked me, "Who's going to play the keyboard?"

I looked at my child seriously and said, "God said you're going to play."

I got the most startled look I've ever seen. Most of my children are musically inclined. This particular child had been playing and tapping around on the keyboard since they were five years old. Everyone saw the gift. My child had led in worship before while singing, but this was the first time leading while playing the piano, so I understood the nervousness. We connected with a friend who played skillfully. She taught my child about twenty-six songs, and my child played skillfully at the conference. There was a mighty rejoicing over what God had done, and what God had spoken came to pass right before our eyes.

At the end, in the midst of everything, we experienced the blessings of the Lord. The teaching and preaching was good, the music was great, and the people were expressing that they were having a good time. Then something went wrong. Someone did something that wasn't in the contract, although we had one more night, some of the management wanted to put us out. They asked for whoever was in charge to come to the front desk and pay the bill, or else we had to leave immediately. I went to take care of the complaint and pay. Someone asked me as I was walking up to the desk, "Do you have that kind of money?"

I said, "Don't worry, pray."

They gave me the bill, and I paid it and closed out the debt. We would check out in the morning and be headed back to Saint Louis.

The final thing that happened upon leaving was that the driver got too close to the building and pulled the gutter off, dragging it away without looking back. The miracle of this conference trip to me was that all seven things that went wrong seemed to be of concern only to me. The people laughed and talked all the way back about what a blessed time they had and how they would definitely go to the next one.

STATEMENTS OF TRUTH

1. When the Lord tells you to do something, don't overthink it, just do it. If you never move, things will never happen.
2. Don't think you've made a mistake because things start to go wrong. When challenges show up, we have to keep moving in faith.
3. Don't think that because God gives you a project everything will go smoothly. Remain positive.

4. Don't lose faith and say, "I made a mistake, God wouldn't put me in this situation." Remember biblical examples like Jonah. The Lord will assign us to some things we don't want to do.

5. When we try to find other ways to obey God, we learn there are no other ways except what He has called us to. Be obedient to God's call, and He will be glorified.

6. Leading a group means being in charge of everything from transportation to setting the stage and bringing in all necessary items. Stay prayerful, keep people safe, and ensure you are covered financially.

Chapter Eighteen

GUIDED BY FAITH

When the Lord comes into our lives, He guides us, and we must listen. When one of my sons was twelve years old, he experienced guidance in a remarkable way. He had recently received Jesus into his life, and he was playing street football with some friends. While trying to think through his next move, he stated that he heard a voice say, "Let Jim take your place." So, he asked Jim if he would take his place, and Jim said yes. As the game moved on, they scored because Jim knew how to make that move, but my son did not. I asked him what would have happened if Jim hadn't switched places with him. He said, "Oh, I would have gotten smashed." This simple act of obedience to God's voice not only protected him but also contributed to their team's success.

STATEMENTS OF TRUTH

1. When the Lord comes into our lives, there are many things that He will do for us.

2. There are two things in particular that He will do. John 16:13 says, "Howbeit when he, the Spirit of truth, is come, he will guide you into all truth."

3. He will comfort you. John 14:26 says, "But the Comforter, which is the Holy Ghost, whom the Father will send in my name, he shall teach you all things, and bring all things to your remembrance, whatsoever I have said unto you."

4. No matter how old a person is in the Lord, God will deal with them on their level so that they may understand His will and purpose.

Chapter Nineteen

A CAUTIONARY TALE OF THE RUBY SHOES

Years ago, I had a peculiar experience involving a pair of shoes. On a Sunday morning, I arrived at the church and found a shoe box at the front door. Inside were a pair of shoes that matched the style I loved to wear with my suits and ministering attire. Excitedly, I discovered they were brand new and in my exact size. Without hesitation, I put on the right shoe. Later, I went to my office and called my mom to share the news. She got quiet and then warned me, "Don't put your foot in that shoe." Unfortunately, I had already worn it, and soon after, my right foot started troubling me. Despite wrapping it and trying various remedies, I began to walk with a limp.

A pastor friend suggested I buy a pair of Nike gym shoes from Shoe Carnival and tie them up tightly. I did so, and with continuous prayer, the condition eventually left just as mysteriously as it had come. This experience taught me the importance of walking carefully and being vigilant in our spiritual journey. The Bible reminds us in Ephesians 5:15–17 to "walk circumspectly, not as fools, but as wise, Redeeming the time, because the days are evil. Wherefore be ye not unwise, but understanding what the will of the Lord is."

To this day, I have no idea who sent those shoes or how they knew my size. It was a lesson to always be cautious and prayerful, ensuring we are not deceived by appearances.

STATEMENTS OF TRUTH

The Word of God teaches us to walk carefully and pay attention in this life. Sometimes we don't realize how important this is until we face a mishap. We should always be careful and walk circumspectly, praying about everything, knowing that the Lord will help us in this walk and in this world. He called us into His marvelous light to work in His vineyard, to do good always and not practice evil because it is the will of God in Christ Jesus concerning us.

1. Every gift you receive isn't from God, even if it looks like it. When my mom told me not to put my foot in the shoes, I had already done it, but I didn't tell her. I learned that if people hate you and can't control you, some will do or say anything to harm you. Some people practice witchcraft. Witchcraft can't harm a believer, but if we know that people practice it, we should pray, and God will reveal it.

Sometimes we have to suffer the evil that people practice on us to expose it.

2. If the shoe fits, wear it. This is a saying I've heard for years, but it was not true in this case. There was some learning in this experience.

3. Watch out for what arrives at your door. My distraction was the new shoes. I didn't know the name-brand Ruby existed, but someone knew and made sure I got a pair. The next distraction was my favorite type of shoe, and someone noticed that. We're not perfect, but we serve a perfect God. Sometimes He allows us to face battles we don't know how to fight. If it wasn't for the experience, I wouldn't have the story to tell.

All of us have enemies. If we are believers, sometimes the people we think are our enemies are not. Meanwhile, the real enemies are moving in and seeking whom they may devour (1 Pet 5:8). I put my right foot in the shoe, falling into a trap without thinking. But I came out of it with the knowledge to continue to pray without ceasing and to give thanks in everything. The healing came through something as simple as going to Shoe Carnival to purchase a pair of Nike gym shoes. I walked to my healing.

Chapter Twenty

A KNOCK AT DAWN

Awakened from a deep sleep at 5:07 a.m. on Monday, April 24th, 2023, I heard a loud knock on my bedroom door. Startled, I said, "Yes!" but there was no response. I knew it wasn't my husband because he was asleep in another room, having been under hospice care since January of 2023. I lay there for about a minute, trying to figure out the incident, and noticed the time: 5:08 a.m. Everything seemed normal afterward.

However, on Thursday, April 27th, in the evening hours, I started feeling extremely tired, barely able to put one foot in front of the other. My blood pressure soared into the two hundreds and kept rising, with the bottom number over one hundred. My heart rate plummeted to forty, accompanied by strong palpitations. I had never experienced anything like this, and I realized I needed help when my heart rate dropped to thirty-eight.

I drove myself to a Total Care Clinic. Test results revealed a blood clot in my lungs, and my blood pressure remained high. The clinic called an ambulance, and despite their efforts, my numbers wouldn't stabilize. One nurse placed two pads on my sides, one on each side. When one of my children asked her about it, she didn't answer but assured me, "We're not trying to scare you; we're trying to keep you safe."

Then, a nurse practitioner came in and said, "Mrs. Harvey, we've found a solution to your problem. It's good news; you need a pacemaker."

Surprised, I responded, "That doesn't sound like good news."

She asked, "Why not?"

I replied, "Don't they have to cut me for that?"

She didn't answer directly but said it would fix my heart rate and improve my blood pressure.

I stayed overnight, from April 27th to the 28th, having breakfast, lunch, and dinner the next day. I felt hopeful that the Lord would give me a divine healing. While I was enjoying a visit from a pastor and minister friends, a team of doctors came in and announced, "Mrs. Harvey, we're here to take you down for your pacemaker." Stunned and numb, I realized God's plan for me was different this time.

The pacemaker was the small Micra model, about the size of a AAA battery. But my body needed time to adjust. Initially, I still felt tired, but after a couple of months, things began to feel more normal. My blood pressure improved dramatically to 110-80

Interestingly, that Monday, my daughter's friend had told her, "I'm praying for your dad, but today God told me to pray for your mother." There's much to be said about the knock on the door. The devil may try to harm you even in your sleep, but remember, you're not going anywhere until it's your time. Trust God every day and leave the results to Him, because He already knows what He will do.

STATEMENTS OF TRUTH

1. Trust in God's timing; the devil may try to harm us, but we are not going anywhere until it is our time. God protects us even in our sleep, ensuring our safety and well-being.
2. When faced with unexpected challenges, maintain faith and believe in God's plan.
3. God can work through medical interventions, such as the pacemaker, to restore health and normalcy.
4. The prayers of others can be a powerful force in our lives, as shown by my daughter's friend's timely intercession.
5. God's plan is perfect; even when things don't go as we expect, He guides us through every step.

Chapter Twenty-One

A PROPHETIC ENCOUNTER: MEETING LIFE-CHANGING PEOPLE

In the 1980s, a woman of God who carried the office of prophetess spoke a powerful word into my life during a casual conversation. She suddenly shifted the topic and said something that I've never forgotten. Paraphrasing her words, she said, "You will meet some people in your future who will change your life. You will be promoted with them."

I believed in her prophecy because she had spoken into my life before, and her words had come to pass. As I continued through life, her prophetic declaration came true once again.

As a prophetic dreamer, I've learned that if God is leading you on paths unknown to you, He knows how to get you where He's taking you. Trust in His guidance, and be open to the people He brings into your life.

STATEMENTS OF TRUTH

1. God sends His people on assignments. Be willing to go.
2. God chooses us for His purpose (Rom 8:28).
3. Some things that the Lord shows and tells us can be scary. But remember, we walk by faith and not by sight.
4. Prepare yourself for the journey and be ready to move out no matter what the words of the prophet look like to you.

Chapter Twenty-Two

A DIFFERENT KIND OF CHURCH EXPERIENCE

On January 1st, 1986, my husband and I felt the call to open our first church. By Easter, we had about fifty youths gathered in the basement of our home, and we taught them the Word of God. Starting a Spirit-filled church, where God is leading and guiding, is not an easy process. First of all, you are called by God to do it, and the devil doesn't like the idea of souls being won for the Kingdom of God.

Soon, we had a full Sunday school in our basement, and the children, one by one, began to give their lives to Jesus by repenting of their sins and asking God to fill them with the Holy Ghost according to Acts 2:38. When the Lord is invited to fill our churches with His power, we will see a great move of God, and we did see that. The children were also taught to honor and respect the Lord, and as we taught these things, we showed them by being an example of these truths. They learned that disrespect to the Word of God could bring judgment to anyone who deliberately disobeyed.

The House of God is where we honor God, worship, and praise Him. It is the House of Prayer. Some tragic things happened here and there because some people didn't take worship seriously. Thanks to the Lord God, His mercies endures forever. The people learned how to truly worship God.

STATEMENTS OF TRUTH

1. Knowing the truth will make you free (John 8:32).
2. "Train up a child in the way he should go: and when he is old, he will not depart from it" (Prov 22:6). Children sometimes stray away from God. When they have been trained in the Word of God, pray and trust the Lord to bring them back. In due season, they will return.
3. It is our duty to continue to win souls for the Lord. It is His will for people to be saved. 2 Peter 3:9 says that the Lord is "not willing that any should perish, but that all should come to repentance."
4. Spirit-filled churches are different and have the Spirit of God in them because the people have accepted the Lord Jesus Christ, have been filled with His Holy Spirit, and do the works of God.
5. The Lord gives his people the power to witness to those who don't know Him (Acts 1:8).

Chapter Twenty-Three

THE HAT INCIDENT: FACING DARK POWERS

I was at an event and sitting at one of the tables when I noticed my head suddenly started to hurt. It felt like my hat was tightening around my head. My first thought was to take it off, but then I heard the Spirit say, "Don't take your hat off." Looking around the room, I noticed a person acting strangely. She had her eyes closed tightly and was repeatedly moving her neck to the left as if in deep concentration. It had been said that she dealt in witchcraft. Meanwhile, my hat continued to feel tighter.

Despite the discomfort, I remembered that we shouldn't be afraid of any evil that anyone desires to harm us with. My head had been fine when I'd left home, and the hat wasn't tight at all. Growing up, I heard that people with dark powers can't hurt you if you don't believe in them. I can't say that the Lord won't allow us to experience the dark side of people if they operate that way, and I know that these kinds of spirits showed up in the Bible—the Apostle Paul even dealt with them (Acts 16:16–17).

When I heard God say, "Don't take your hat off," I chose to ignore what the woman was doing. Eventually, she stopped, and the pressure on my head eased.

STATEMENTS OF TRUTH

1. In negative situations, "resist the devil, and he will flee from you" (Jas 4:7).
2. Avoid being fearful, because that's not the spirit that the Lord gave us. 2 Timothy 1:7 says, "For God hath not given us a spirit of fear; but of power and of love and of a sound mind."
3. Pray for those who desire to harm you that they may be healed.
4. Not everybody will experience these things because their assignments are different. Some people have said that they're not interested in dealing with these types of things, but it is possible for these things to show up when working for the Lord.
5. Be ready at all times, because we don't know when we'll meet up with something unexpected. The only thing you can do is pray and keep a pure heart before God, and He'll fight for you.
6. Jesus experienced the dark side, and so did the apostles.

Chapter Twenty-Four

KIDNAPPED FROM THE PORCH

When one of my children was about five years old, they went outside to play on the porch while other children were also playing nearby. I was doing housework when I went to the window and noticed the child was missing. I immediately went outside and asked if anyone had seen anything, but everyone said no. People in the area started calling out, but there was no response.

Feeling desperate, I went inside, fell to my knees, and prayed, asking the Lord to fix the situation and send my child home. I prayed for protection and deliverance in the name of Jesus. After my prayer, I went back outside and, almost immediately, the Lord sent the victory. My child came running from the back of a neighbor's house. It was a moment of immense relief and joy, and I praised God that it didn't turn into a horror story.

STATEMENTS OF TRUTH

1. Prayer works; when trouble shows up, immediate deliverance isn't always guaranteed, but prayer is powerful. 1 John 5:14–15 says, "And this is the confidence that we have in him, that if we ask anything according to his will, he heareth us. And if we know that he hear us whatsoever we ask, we know that we have the petitions that we desired of him."

2. Trust in Jesus; when we can't figure out a situation, turning to Jesus in prayer is the best solution. He knows what to do and will fix it for us.

3. As parents, we must be vigilant. This situation is a reminder that we can't always trust a child to stay in a safe place. Children can easily get distracted and move on their own. In any trouble, always pray. Luke 18:1b says, "Men ought always to pray, and not to faint."

Chapter Twenty-Five

TRAGIC CHOICES: A YOUNG DRUG DEALER'S STORY

I met a young man years ago and introduced him to Jesus, and he became a part of our ministry. After a while, he left the ministry and went back into the world. It was said that he became a drug dealer. A few years passed, but I felt a strong need to speak with him. One day, he called me.

I told him that the Lord had a better plan for him. He responded, "You mean to tell me you're asking me to give up making $9,000 a day to go to McDonald's and make minimum wage to follow Jesus?"

I replied, "I'm only telling you that if you accept Jesus into your life, your life will change, and you'll trust God to take care of you." Unfortunately, he couldn't do it, and he died in that condition.

He reminded me of the rich young ruler in Matthew 19:16–24, who came to Jesus and asked, "Good Master, what good thing shall I do, that I may have eternal life?" Jesus started quoting the commandments to him, and the young man said, "All these things I have kept from my youth up: what lack I yet?"

In verse 21, Jesus replied, "If thou will be perfect, go and sell that thou hast, and give to the poor, and thou shalt have treasure in heaven, and come and follow me." In verse 22, we read that the young man went away sorrowful, for he had great possessions. Like the young drug dealer, he just couldn't do it.

STATEMENTS OF TRUTH

1. Jesus said it is the Father who draws people to Jesus (John 6:44).
2. The Lord said in Matthew 11:28, "Come unto me all ye that labour and are heavy laden, and I will give you rest."
3. "Behold, I stand at the door, and knock: if any man hear my voice, and open the door, I will come in to him, and will sup with him, and he with me" (Rev 3:20).

Chapter Twenty-Six

DIVINE PROTECTION FROM POISON

Years ago, some food was dropped off at our home. Everyone who ate the food got mildly sick, while those who did not eat it were fine. We later discovered that the food had been poisoned. Despite the discomfort, we were all grateful for God's protection and the revelation of the truth.

STATEMENTS OF TRUTH

1. We experienced divine protection. "And these signs shall follow them that believe....and if they drink any deadly thing, it shall not hurt them" (Mark 16:17–18). This promise to believers was evident in our experience.

2. God's goodness was shown in how He revealed the truth about the poisoned food and protected us from serious harm.

Chapter Twenty-Seven

HEALED FROM DEADLY ALLERGIES

One day we noticed that my daughter would have an allergic reaction to just about anything and everything that she ate. We took her to a specialist, but they couldn't determine what was causing it. Sometimes we would go out and she would react from eating a candy bar, an ice cream cone, or different kinds of foods, even vegetables. It got so bad that it started shutting her breathing off, and we would be on our way to the ER over and over again.

Early one morning, I was praying about these allergies, and the Lord led me to go into her room and lay hands on her that she might receive her healing in the name of Jesus. As I obeyed the Spirit of God and laid hands on her, she became really still. I asked her later about the stillness, and she said, "Oh, I was afraid. I was repenting, because your voice changed and sounded like the voice of many waters." From that day on, she was healed and never had another attack. When she was having those attacks, we prayed hard, because it appeared that we were going to lose her. But thanks be to God, He already knew what He would do.

STATEMENTS OF TRUTH

1. Although the Lord saves His people, we are still subject to sickness. We can take our sicknesses to the Lord, and He will heal us. We were already praying for her healing, but that last prayer, God anointed me to go harder into prayer. I knew what she meant about the voice of many waters because I heard it. God healed her, and the next morning she was eating everything that was prepared. It has been over forty years, and she's still healed.

2. We must come to Jesus in faith. If He doesn't show up in the first prayer, keep praying and believing; we can't afford to give up. In addition, the one you are praying for must have faith as well. Hebrews 11:6 says, "But without faith it is impossible to please him: for he that cometh to God must believe that he is, and that he is a rewarder of them that diligently seek him."

Chapter Twenty-Eight

STANDING FIRM
THROUGH TRIALS

These incidents happened years ago, but they happened. I'm writing these stories that the Lord is revealing to me because many of them I had forgotten about. Some of you may be familiar with these types of tests—they've become testimonies to other people who don't know how to suffer on that level. We need to learn personally what the Lord is saying to those who love Him. Matthew 7:12 says, "Therefore all things whatsoever ye would that men should do to you, do ye even so to them." Simply treat others the way you want to be treated. Tell Jesus about it: "Casting all your care upon him, for he careth for you" (1 Pet 5:7).

We must learn to think the way Jesus thought: "Let this mind be in you, which was also in Christ Jesus" (Phil 2:5). Learn how to do what the

Word of God is saying: "Be ye doers of the Word and not hearers only, deceiving your own selves" (Jas 1:22). This is how we put the Word of God into practice. We must learn to pursue peace with all men and holiness without which no man shall see the Lord. We can keep this in mind when we're in conflict with other people; whatever situation we find ourselves in, we must pursue in peace and love.

Understand this: not everyone is looking for someone to pick on. We know that people are different. Some folks wouldn't waste their time picking on others, and others will. Remember Joseph? The Bible says his brothers hated him and sought to destroy him. One day they thought they had gotten rid of him. Many years later, Pharaoh had promoted him. The brothers who hated him had to go to Egypt with their father for food. Although the brothers who had hated him had come for food, they were so spiritually blind that they didn't see this was their brother whom they had mistreated and hated. Now they needed him, and if he wouldn't help them, they would starve. This is why we have to stay connected to the Word of God and always do the right things.

Don't destroy your integrity trying to defend yourself. Don't try to get even. Be encouraged by these verses from Romans 12: "Be not overcome of evil, but overcome evil with good" (Rom 12:21). "Vengeance is mine; I will repay, saith the Lord" (Rom 12:19). "If it be possible, as much as lieth in you, live peaceably with all men" (Rom 12:18). "Be of the same mind one toward another" (Rom 12:16). "Bless them which persecute you: bless, and curse not" (Rom 12:14). "Be kindly affectioned one to another with brotherly love; in honour preferring one another" (Rom 12:10). "Cleave to that which is good" (Rom 12:9).

STATEMENTS OF TRUTH

1. 2 Peter 1:8 says, "For if these things be in you and abound, they make you that ye shall neither be barren nor unfruitful in the knowledge of our Lord Jesus Christ. But he that lacketh these things is blind and cannot see afar off, and hath forgotten that he was purged from his old sins." The whole chapter confirms all of this.
2. We can't afford to forget how the Word of God teaches us how to be, act, and react to negative situations. As we continue to remember and do what the Word says, we continue with our new life that God has given to us.
3. No one understands that there are many good things we have experienced in our lives along with the bad. All of it was necessary, or the Lord wouldn't have allowed us to go through it. To God be the glory for all of it, because God allows it to make us better and not bitter.

Conclusion

I hope all who reads this book will draw strength and courage from these stories. If you're a dreamer, pay attention to your dreams, because many times, God deals with people in dreams or tells us things in dreams. In most of the dreams in this book God was showing me how to handle things that would come to pass. He was also showing me how to act in situations that I wasn't knowledgeable of, and things He wanted me to know. I have heard people say that they are not dreamers, but whether we dream or not, God knows how to get our attention so that we will understand what He's saying to us.

Life can be frightening sometimes, especially when it comes to going through things we have never experienced before. When this happens, the best thing to do is go to the Lord, pray, and ask Him to help us through it. We must ask Him to show us how, and always trust what His Word says. He will continue to rescue us over and over again.

Everyone goes through tests and trials more than once or twice in this life. People in general, and Christians specifically, don't escape this; the Word of God details the many things the early Church suffered. We must be steadfast in our faith, and no matter what happens, we must not give up.

We'll have many experiences in life, and many of them will turn into life lessons if we allow them to. At other times, we will just draw a blank and not know what to do. During those times, God will often send a prophetic message to build us up and strengthen our faith so we can keep moving. The Lord does not desire for us to be defeated because of the tests and trials we may go through. He will keep sending people to encourage us through life, and eventually, we'll be anchored to help others through rough places.

Acknowledgments

I am so grateful that the Lord chose me to write this book, and I thank Him for the seven witnesses that He sent to confirm the writing. I want to personally thank all the seven witnesses, as they were so special on my journey and spoke prophetically. They are: Dr. Faith Joshua, Prophetess Sheila Coleman, Evangelist Jannette Green, Sis. Tabitha Cheairs, Bro. Marvis Harvey, Bro. Cedric M. Smith, and Elect Lady Irma Carter and thank you to proofreader, LaVerne Sandidge MBA. Your support and encouragement has been with me all the way. Thank you to all of my supportive family and friends—I appreciate you all. To God be the glory for all He has done!

Author Biography

Dr. Ruby J. Harvey works diligently in Christian ministry. In March 1996, Dr. Harvey founded ICAM (I Care About Myself) Ministries centered around helping people with low self-esteem, inner hurts, pain from the past, and much more. Many people have been delivered through this ministry.

Dr. Harvey has been preaching and teaching the Word of God for over forty-one years. She obtained a master's degree in Christian Counseling from International Bible College and a doctorate from Saints Academy Bible College. Currently, she resides with her family in Saint Louis, Missouri, and is involved in outreach and Christian growth ministries.

CONTACT INFORMATION

- Facebook: Ruby Harvey Ministries
- Email: drrubyjay@gmail.com
- Website: http://www.drrubyharvey.com
- Phone: 314-418-9621